"We are used to thinking of religion as mainly a force for tradition; this book is a timely and sprightly reminder that it can be a springboard for change as well, as long as we're willing to reimagine the contemporary meaning of our deep roots."

BILL MCKIBBEN, author of *The Flag, the Cross, and the Station Wagon*

"*Tending Tomorrow* is a visionary call to action, inviting readers on a transformative journey toward a sustainable and equitable future. Merging real-life stories with deep, communal engagement, this book encourages us to reimagine our relationship with the world and our spiritual and cultural roots. It addresses the despair and hopelessness many feel in the face of polycrisis, offering a beacon of hope. Through its pages, we are guided to redream, retell, and renew our collective destiny, making it an essential read for anyone seeking hope and direction in challenging times."

HYUNG JIN KIM SUN, senior leader for antiracism and intercultural conciliation for CRCNA and author of *Who Are Our Enemies and How Do We Love Them?*

"Leah Reesor-Keller weaves an intelligent and relatable vision for courageous honesty and compassionate action when faced with what truth and reconciliation ask of us. As a mother, an activist, and a Christian, she shares a pathway that can inspire our own as we collectively awaken to the challenges by radically grounding our lives in Reality rather than denial and Love rather than fear."

VICTORIA LOORZ, founder of the Center for Wild Spirituality, cofounder of the Wild Church network, and author of *Church of the Wild: How Nature Invites Us into the Sacred*

"*Tending Tomorrow* is more than a book; it is a must-read and a call to action for anyone seeking inspiration and practical steps to contribute to a healthier planet. Leah Reesor-Keller inspires readers to engage in foundational practices that go beyond rhetoric, fostering real and positive change. By digging into the roots of faith and culture, we discover the potential to repair injustice and sow seeds for a better tomorrow. This book beautifully weaves together spirituality and ecological responsibility. Reesor-Keller's insights provide a powerful appeal, urging those ready to answer to be courageous stewards of both people and the planet."

DOROTHY NYAMBI, president and CEO of Mennonite Economic Development Associates

"In a book rich with personal stories and clear challenges, Leah Reesor-Keller accomplishes her task—guiding us in the resetting of our collective values, beliefs, and practices, moving us all toward a healthier future in which all that the Spirit sustains can thrive."

DOUG KLASSEN, executive minister of Mennonite Church Canada

"Writing with a confidence and candor only experience can produce, Leah Reesor-Keller shows a path to the future. This book moves key conversations in the right direction."

ANTHONY SIEGRIST, Ontario director for A Rocha Canada and author of *Speaking of God: An Essential Guide to Christian Thought*

TENDING TOMORROW

TENDING TOMORROW

COURAGEOUS CHANGE
for **PEOPLE** *and* **PLANET**

Leah Reesor-Keller

FOREWORD BY
JOHN PAUL LEDERACH

HERALD
P R E S S

Harrisonburg, Virginia

Herald Press
PO Box 866, Harrisonburg, Virginia 22803
www.HeraldPress.com

Library of Congress Cataloging-in-Publication Data
Names: Reesor-Keller, Leah, author.
Title: Tending tomorrow : courageous change for people and planet / Leah
  Reesor-Keller.
Description: Harrisonburg : Herald Press, 2024. | Includes bibliographical
  references.
Identifiers: LCCN 2024003916 (print) | LCCN 2024003917 (ebook) | ISBN
  9781513813356 (paperback) | ISBN 9781513813363 (hardcover) | ISBN
  9781513813370 (ebook)
Subjects: LCSH: Human ecology--Religious aspects--Christianity. |
  Ecology--Religious aspects--Christianity. | Ecotheology. | Climatic
  changes--Religious aspects--Christianity. | BISAC: RELIGION / Christian
  Living / Social Issues | RELIGION / Leadership
Classification: LCC HT695.5 R44 2024 (print) | LCC HT695.5 (ebook) | DDC
  261.8/8--dc23/eng/20240227
LC record available at https://lccn.loc.gov/2024003916
LC ebook record available at https://lccn.loc.gov/2024003917

Study guides are available for many Herald Press titles at www.HeraldPress.com.

TENDING TOMORROW
© 2024 by Herald Press, Harrisonburg, Virginia 22803. 800-245-7894. All rights reserved.
Library of Congress Control Number: 2024003916
International Standard Book Number: 978-1-5138-1335-6 (paperback);
    978-1-5138-1336-3 (hardcover); 978-1-5138-1337-0 (ebooks)
Vines: Yuliya Ranchanka / iStock / Getty Images Plus
Printed in United States of America

All rights reserved. This publication may not be reproduced, stored in a retrieval system, or
transmitted in whole or in part, in any form, by any means, electronic, mechanical, photo-
copying, recording or otherwise without prior permission of the copyright owners.
Scripture quotations, unless otherwise noted, are from New Revised Standard Version Bible
Updated Edition. Copyright © 2021 National Council of Churches of Christ in the United
States of America. Used by permission. All rights reserved worldwide.

28 27 26 25 24   10 9 8 7 6 5 4 3 2 1

CONTENTS

For Ava and Isaac

FOREWORD

i.

Tending tomorrow is such an evocative image.

To imagine the days that unfold before us and before our grandchildren and before our yet-to-be-born as a garden. With its soils, seeds, plants, and harvests across seasons and generations, this garden offers openness and potential and an everlasting invitation to come alongside.

And.

This was the first joy I found in Leah Reesor-Keller's life and writing. In *Tending Tomorrow*, her sense of expansive imagination—the living for *and* flourishing now—offers little space to narrowness, exclusion, and the tyrannies of either/or binaries.

Leah evokes our imagination. She invites us to notice what is here in new ways. She asks us to walk toward the emergent with a sense of awe and courage.

Maybe this is why as children we sang about rivers running *deep and wide* and never about rivers that ran shallow and restricted. Something about God's ceaseless and unfolding love kept coming to mind.

ii.

Tending tomorrow is such a poetic image.

Over the past years I had the honor to accompany the Colombian Truth Commission. "Truth Commission" was actually the shorthand version of their name. As it appeared in the national peace accord ending a half-century of war, the authors had a more poetic inclination: the Commission to Bring Light to the Truth, Learn to Live Together, and Never Repeat Violence.

Traveling throughout the country, the head of the Commission, Father Francisco "Pacho" de Roux, and the dozen commissioners often faced the question of how to attend to the harms that dated across generations, if not centuries, and forge the courage to face an uncertain future while knowing that everyone was still living in close proximity to their historic enemies.

Tending Tomorrow journeys along these same pathways, holding the deep tensions of lived harm and appealing to repair, responsibility, and the wells of healing elucidated by Indigenous understanding and nature's extraordinary capacity to call us to respect and healing.

Tending Tomorrow had me thinking of the Argentinian poet Jorge Luis Borges's response to the question of what he thought about hope. "Ah, hope," he is said to have responded, "this lovely memory of the future."

Leah's writing had me pondering what an extraordinary species we truly are, that we humans can recall the past and remember the future.

Perhaps this is the most significant aspect of gardening the future: Hope is not a slippery flight from the realities we have spawned and harmed. Hope is not end-time escapism. Hope is the tilling we do today.

Leah might say hope is wilding.

iii.

Tending tomorrow is such a courageous image.

Leah raises the question: What if church were a river and not a building? Well, that is my way of framing one of her key questions.

Rivers are an example of what the new sciences call a process-structure, these natural phenomena that simultaneously display adaptive dynamism and clarity of structure organized around purpose.

We face a time, well articulated in these chapters, where for many people the forms and structures of church no longer hold their aspirational waters in pursuit of meaningful and responsive expression of spirituality and faith.

Tending Tomorrow opens an extraordinary conversation of courage—to imagine beyond what exists now, knowing that God's love is constant, and to be willing to pursue the creativity needed to unleash the unexpected and then let it flourish.

This kind of courage will require grace.

Grace is far more than leniency or ignoring.

Grace is choosing to live with and into the unknown, something akin to the courage to embody expansive love without fully knowing and seeing.

The author of Hebrews called it *faith*.

Leah calls it church as a movement.

iv.

Tending tomorrow is such a natural image.

I share a love for Nepal with Leah. My journeys came alongside local and national leaders during and after the civil war. Among those were the people who first initiated the idea of community-based forest user groups. There is a tender tenacity that rises from people whose livelihoods gather around the well-being of a local forest, and enough of them gather to become the de facto national ministry of forestry.

Among the things I learned from forest user groups were their originating principles.

You join the movement by joining a local group responsible for a local forest.

You cannot form a new local forest-user chapter unless that chapter is half women and half men.

Everyone proximate and connected to the forest is welcome to join, no matter their caste or color.

Everyone.

From my conversations, the forest-user movement started with a dozen or so originators. It now has more than seven million participants.

It is amazing what happens when you are accompanied by and learn from the Forest as a teacher.

Neles Tebay, a Catholic priest from Papua, once shared with me the proverb he learned as a child from his father. *The Forest accepts all people.*

Leah would call it *beloved of God in all manifestations.*

v.

Tending tomorrow is such a wondrous first and last line of a haiku.

I write haiku. I listen in haiku.

I find this form of writing poetry meditative. Prayerful.

Leah's book reminded me of haiku-as-prayer.

Chapters short. Ideas clear. Meditation deep.

A haiku I wrote earlier this year—this year nearly a quarter of a century into the century when we will decide whether

and how we will garden our future—came to mind as ending
words for a foreword for this book everyone should read.

> *morning sun traces*
> *spiders' night moves holding the*
> *garden together*

—**John Paul Lederach,** professor of international
peacebuilding at the University of Notre Dame,
Distinguished Scholar at Eastern Mennonite
University, and author of *Reconcile: Conflict
Transformation for Ordinary Christians*

PREFACE

Religion is above all an ongoing process of meaning-making. Religion is interpretation all the way down. As its Latin roots in religare *("re-bind," "re-member," "re-connect") and* relegere *("re-read") suggest, religion is reading and rereading, connecting and reconnecting, imaginatively re-membering our world. It is fundamentally about creatively reinterpreting and remaking inherited traditions—scriptures, ideas, beliefs, practices and institutions—in light of new and emerging horizons of meaning.*

—**Timothy Beal,** *When Time Is Short*[1]

In my Anabaptist-Mennonite branch of the Christian tradition, handed down in my family over five hundred years, we value the freedom of new revelation.[2] Often called the movement of the Spirit, this belief creates space for changing understandings as we humans face new contexts that our spiritual ancestors never imagined. This kind of meaning-making—of reinterpreting and remaking inherited traditions—is the work of this book. In these pages, I turn to my culture and faith tradition to imagine new paths of meaning to meet the context of our time.

It is cliché to say that the world is changing around us, for that is the nature of the world—things change. Time's river flows, and we move with its currents. In the past few years, we've experienced a global pandemic, wars in multiple continents, and shifts in global political and economic power from the Global North to rising influence of China, India, and other growing powers on the world stage. Movements for gender justice, civil rights, and Indigenous sovereignty have surged, as have rising authoritarian tendencies and strongman politics. The backdrop to these human-centered activities is the looming specter of climate change, with impacts like droughts, floods, wildfires, and high-intensity storms already being felt around the world

The role of churches and religious institutions is changing, especially in the two countries where I am a citizen, Canada and the United States. Christian nationalist movements are on the rise, and mainline denominations are rapidly shrinking. Christianity is growing globally, including in my own tradition, where there are now more Anabaptist-Mennonites in Africa, Asia, and South America than in North America and Europe.

Christian theology—that is, thinking about the nature of the divine and practices of religious beliefs—can be understood only through the lived reality of our human experiences. It must continually be made and remade in the context of our changing world. "Our theology has changed across generations and geography," writes Hyung Jin Kim Sun, an ordained Mennonite pastor and scholar of intercultural theology. "And it needs to continue to change as we seek theological perspectives that resonate with the new reality of a church that has become more global and more diverse than ever."[3]

Kim Sun calls on the Anabaptist-Mennonite tradition to take an intercultural approach centered in mutuality and genuine engagement with other perspectives and traditions. In other words, this requires us, says Kim Sun, "to engage deeply, with an attitude that our perspective is limited and we can learn from others."[4]

Following Kim Sun's call to engage deeply with a learning attitude, I am going back to the roots of my inherited faith tradition and culture, looking to bring diverse perspectives to bear on what it means to believe and act—to live—in a way that leads to the well-being and flourishing of all people, and of all creation. In this book, I dig into the roots of my inherited faith and cultural tradition in order to redream it in the context that I live in today. There are five thematic actions: redreaming, retelling, renewing, reimagining, and rewilding. While these actions are more interconnected than sequential, I've set them in this order to show the flow from beliefs to actions to future hopes for flourishing. Beliefs and values examined in the earlier chapters are expressed in practices in the later chapters, mirroring how cultures are complex accumulations of values and beliefs which are expressed in our actions and in our forms of organizing in institutions and communities.

This book is an offering of hope to my Christian faith tradition and beyond. It is a vision of how we might adapt and change as people looking to live well together and in harmony with the natural world, finding meaning in new and old ways to sustain ourselves and our descendants in the coming decades and unimaginable centuries and millennia ahead. This book is not an exhaustive treatise on the only way, or the best way, forward. I offer my journey of meaning-making as a jumping-off point for making sense of your own experiences, values, and beliefs. Your story and faith tradition may follow a different path than mine, but I hope you will recognize within my journey shared here some of your own struggles, longings, and hopes for a better future for everyone and for our planet.

I pray that reading this book is a heart journey, a meandering path navigating the complexities and challenges of holding on to hope—of being people of hope—in this time when it feels like the world is on fire. And it is a journey best undertaken with others. I hope that you will find conversation partners in book club meetings, Sunday school discussions, and college classrooms. Questions at the back of the book offer ideas for contemplation and conversation. I encourage you to think about what these ideas mean to you, and how you might apply them and add your own imaginings and lived experiences to find inspiration for making courageous change. So start small, dream big, and hold space for what liberatory, flourishing things may emerge.

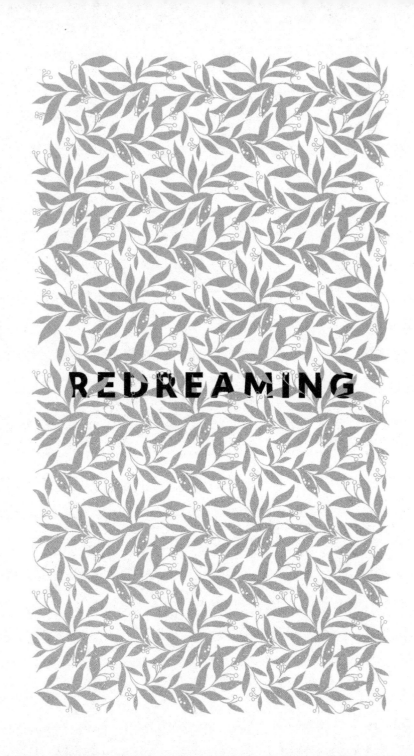

REDREAMING

1

REDREAMING AT
THE ROOTS

I set *The Sixth Extinction* and *The Weather of the Future* on the highest shelf in the living room, level with my eyeline and well above a child's line of vision. Did Isaac see them? Would he be curious about these library books I'd just brought home? My seven-year-old is turning into a hungry reader like I was at his age. We've been reading books together about the universe's deep expanse that births galaxies and black holes, about wind, gravity, and tectonic forces shaping the earth through the geological eras. Lying on my son's denim patchwork quilt at bedtime, I read Isaac the creation story in Genesis alongside articles in children's science magazines with descriptions of the Big Bang and the slow miracles of life emerging and diversifying over the millennia on our planet. He knows that the earth is warming and that human activities—like throwing trash in the oceans, paving over animal habitats, and using fossil fuels—are harming the planet. In science class he watches videos about smog. But does he understand the scope of the changes we are living through on our blue planet, and what it will mean for all our futures? The global warming scenarios for the year

2100 from the Intergovernmental Panel on Climate Change fall within Isaac's lifetime. Human-driven climate change and ecological destruction are already wreaking havoc through droughts, storms, floods, fires, and the economic and political instability of conflict over natural resources.[1] Does my son know we are teetering on tipping points, perhaps already past them, for irreversible changes?

Isaac knows that the world—the universe—is beautiful, intricate, and full of wonder. My spouse and I chose Isaac's name for its meaning of joy and laughter. Does he already know that he is also inheriting a world full of grief and loss? I want to prepare him, because I believe that the theme of grief will be part of his life over and over in the years ahead. I anticipate that the coming years will be marked by escalating climate chaos, rising inequalities, and high levels of conflict and sociopolitical instability in Canada where we live and around the world. My child will need courage in his life ahead, just as those of us who are adults now need courage to imagine and take action toward change so we can move away from the path of destruction we are on.

Scientists call this unfolding moment in geological history the Anthropocene, an era in which human-driven activity has had an observable impact on the earth. Which humans? Which activities? The advent of the Anthropocene is linked to the rise of the Industrial Revolution, is inextricably connected to the trans-Atlantic slave trade and the genocide and displacement of Indigenous Peoples, and is undergirded by white supremacist beliefs that used Christianity to justify exploitation of people and planet. Yet as we see over and over again in disasters and crises around the world, the people and countries that have contributed the most to the climate crisis are not the ones experiencing the brunt of the impact.

In 2021, UNICEF reported that one billion children—nearly half the world's children—live in countries that are at extreme risk for climate change impacts, including heat waves, flooding, and diseases like dengue fever. "The highest-risk places on Earth contribute least to the causes of climate change," the agency reported. "The 33 extremely high-risk countries emit less than ten percent of global greenhouse gas emissions. The ten most extremely high-risk countries emit only 0.5 per cent of global emissions."[2] In Canada, we see the impacts of climate change on the most vulnerable as well: the young, the elderly, and the marginalized, including the unhoused, are most likely to experience health issues during climate-related disasters like heat waves and wildfire smoke events.

I say I'm worried about Isaac and his four-year-old sister Ava, but what I really mean is that I'm worried about all of us—myself included—and the future generations to follow us as we anticipate coming critical decades in a world transformed by climatic changes and the societal fallout. For Millennials like me, younger folks in Gen Z, and the children including Isaac and Ava who make up Gen Alpha, climate change is not a niche issue; it is the unfolding story of our embodied lives. I'm worried about the whole world, including the people and places already experiencing the full force of the climate crisis and the violence and displacement that accompany it. We are on a trajectory of death, and I'm worried about how we as the human community can make the kinds of decisions necessary to change it. And whether that trajectory changes or doesn't, we must grapple with how we and future generations will make our home in an inhospitable future.

I am writing about this as though I am a distant observer, someone watching from afar as things happen beyond me. Sometimes it feels like I am watching our future unfold through a TV screen or a mobile news app. Headlines about ice shelf collapse in Antarctica. Images of earth cracked from drought. News reports on the record profits of fossil fuel companies and the banks that fund them. The distance is an illusion, a sign of my privilege to choose apathy over engagement. There are no spectators in our world, only actors making choices consciously or unconsciously that shape our collective future as the human community. We are inseparably linked to each other and to the community of the natural world, the universe in which we live.

My awareness of the breadth and depth of the world and human experience within it began at an early age. I vividly recall sitting on a smooth wooden bench with other children in a rural Haitian church. I am the same age as Isaac. My feet dangle over the reddish packed-earth floor. Above me, the tin roof magnifies the day's heat as we learn Matthew 4:4 by rote in Haitian Creole. "One does not live by bread alone, but by every word that comes from the mouth of God," we chant in unison.

My parents had been guided by their faith to leave our farm and close-knit Swiss Mennonite community in Markham, Ontario, to move to a village in the northeast corner of Haiti to serve as community workers with a Mennonite development organization. Those three years, from when I was six to when I was nine, shaped my worldview and my faith more than any other experience in my life. In Haiti, the country's first democratically elected president, a former Catholic priest, had been ousted in a military coup d'etat. Even in the north-eastern village we lived in, a day's drive from the capital city of Port-au-Prince, violence, repression, and economic scarcity deeply affected people's lives. I saw the church become a bastion of hope. It spoke in coded language about Moses and God's deliverance for God's people against the backdrop of military repression. Hunger was an everyday reality for many. To say that bread alone is not enough to satisfy, and that we need God's liberating Word, was radical. The church proclaimed that human beings are *people*—complex beings loved by God and worthy of dignity, capable of being co-creators with God. We are more than empty mouths seeking subsistence.

Growing up in an environment nurtured by faithful people committed to working for justice, hope, and enough food for all shaped my understanding of what it means to be a committed Christian. I wanted to be part of this movement of God's love and liberation, and I still do today. As an adult, that childhood-instilled desire to be part of God's unfolding love in the world led me to study community development and social movements. I applied and refined what I learned in formal education and in working with churches and social justice organizations in Canada as well as in Jamaica, Haiti, and Nepal.

I believe that true Christian faith bears good fruit and seeks liberation, fullness of life, and flourishing for all. Our churches, our faith communities and organizations, and our movements for change need to be held up to this ethic of embodied love in an unjust and broken world that was created good—and still is. I believe that the Spirit is still moving among us, still inspiring life and possibility, hope and goodness, even amid pain and despair. And I believe that God is with us amid the suffering, that God grieves alongside us for everything that is not as it should be, for each person and species and good thing that was and now is not.

I imagine myself walking through life holding hope in one hand and grief in the other. Jesus' words from John 10:10 echo in my head: "The thief comes only to steal and kill and destroy. I came that they may have life and have it abundantly." This is the longing in all our souls—to have life abundantly, a life and a future of flourishing.

Ecology, the study of interactions among and between organisms and their environment, has given me a new lens to think about how we relate to each other and our environment— how we pursue that abundant life, that future of flourishing. Interconnection and interdependence are foundational to ecological thinking. Human beings are inseparably part of the change processes that make up our planet and universe. And though humans are just one ingredient in the mix, the advent of the Anthropocene demonstrates our species' influence on our planet and beyond. Ancient actions, ancient choices, ancient hierarchies have influenced where we are today, and the actions we take or don't take today spread out possible futures like an array of galaxies before us. *It doesn't have to be this way* is the constant refrain in my head. What might it look like to develop a different set of interactions and relationships among people, a way of *being* out of which a future of flourishing for people and the planet could blossom?

This book is about the *how* of moving together as people of faith toward a good future, about going back to the literal and metaphorical roots and processes that can support many outcomes of liberation in which all creation can thrive. It is about reorienting and grounding ourselves, paying attention to the relationships and culture patterns that we are building, trusting that good things, needed things, liberating things, will emerge from the foundations we are setting in place now.

In her book *Emergent Strategy*, writer and activist adrienne maree brown writes that "what we practice at the small scale sets the patterns for the whole system."[3] To demonstrate the relationship between the small scale and the large scale, brown draws on the imagery of fractals. A fractal pattern looks similar whether it is broken down into small components or viewed as a complete whole. Imagine ice crystals or a snowflake. As you zoom in and look closer at it under a microscope, you see that each part looks like a smaller version of the whole.

In this book, I follow brown's lead in examining the roots of culture in all its fractal elements. By culture, I mean the beliefs, values, and practices that form patterns of interactions from which worldviews, organizations, and systems emerge. This book is organized around these components of culture, starting with the beliefs and values that shape our responses, then applying those to specific practices and imagining how they play out to influence organizations and systems.

This is a journey of coming to terms with the hardship and pain of the world—the groaning of creation—and sustaining ourselves for the marathon of human existence. It's about going back to the roots of faith and culture to reexamine the patterns of our lives and our faith communities. This work will equip us and future generations to keep running this marathon and holding on to hope that a global existence of human and natural thriving is possible and worth fighting for. It's urgent work, and it has been urgent for centuries. It is the work of this moment and the work of our lifetimes, and it will be the work of generations to come. If we want to change the harmful trajectory that we are on, we have to write new stories and reclaim old ones about the church, each other, and about our place as humans in the community of the cosmos.

This work of redreaming at the roots of culture begins with looking at stories we tell about our origins. Stories have narrative power to provide meaning and shape culture. Reexamining how we tell foundational stories, including creation stories and family history stories, helps us name the values and beliefs, conscious and unconscious, that shape us. In light of the hardship and grief of this time of massive changes and loss, drawing on the wisdom of our ancestors (both physical and spiritual) is an important source of strength for the internal journey of navigating the realms of despair and grief. We can't hide from it or ignore it; we must reckon with difficult realities in order to find hope and courage to keep striving for a better world for ourselves and future generations.

The beliefs and values that emerge from retelling origin stories and looking at the strengths of religious tradition form the foundation for reimagining how we come together in communities, organizations, movements, and churches to build patterns of relationships, actions, and interactions for cultivating a flourishing future. What emerges from our systems and structures will be shaped by how and whether we listen to all voices in the community, how power flows and how it is expected to be used, what leadership values and practices are prioritized, and what expectations undergird our accountability practices.

The challenges facing us require expanding our imaginations of what it means to be the church: from a set of institutions to a fluid and agile movement connecting different groups and individuals. The goal is not a new vision or blueprint for one kind of future—written by one kind of person or people—but a rewilding that seeds many possibilities, creating space for different visions of flourishing to take root.

Isaac's seven-year-old life in urban Kitchener, a rapidly growing city in southern Ontario, is a lot different from mine in rural Haiti. Anticipating the decades ahead, I want faith to be a source of strength and grounding direction for him as it has been for me since my childhood. I want him to hear stories, prayers, and songs that sustain him and give him courage to keep dreaming and working toward a future where people and the natural world can thrive together, where everyone has what they need to live in peace and dignity.

To begin, we have to keep believing that something different is possible and that it is worth fighting for. Just as the astounding breadth and variety of life on our planet has emerged through tiny changes accumulated over time, the cultures that we build and practice in our churches and communities today create the conditions for what is to come. We can't control the fruit of our labor, but we can tend the seeds for courageous change.

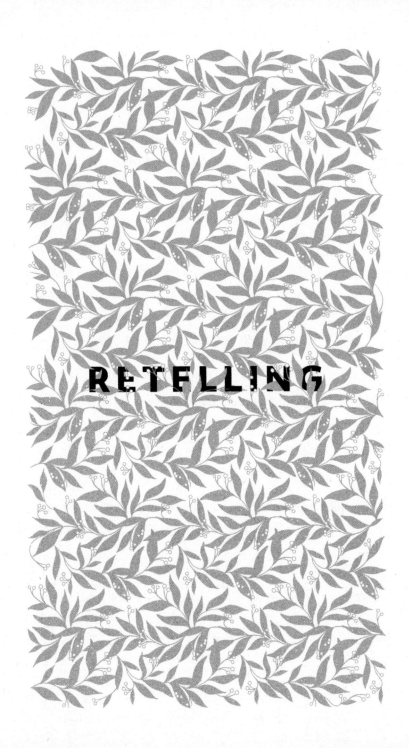

RETELLING

2

RETELLING FAMILY AND SPIRITUAL ANCESTRY STORIES

Courageous change requires a clear understanding of history. Only then can we be intentional in choosing our steps forward. From the stories we tell about ourselves and our place in the world to the records and impact that we leave behind, how we think about the past and our role in it shapes our future. This will look different for each of us. The stories we tell about ourselves shape our values and beliefs and affect how we see ourselves in relation to others. Our history has influenced where we are today in positive and negative ways. Looking carefully at the stories handed down to us, and the meanings that they have been imbued with, can help us find paths forward that draw on the strength of history while imagining a different kind of future that learns from the mistakes of the past. Going back to my family and spiritual ancestry stories, and the unfolding story of the land that I live on, the unfolding story of the earth in this age of human-influenced changes, has helped me shape the values I want to live into and to pass on to my descendants to lead to a better future for all people and our planet home.

A wooden boardwalk winds around the shoreline of Crawford Lake. It creates a smooth walkway over the rugged rocks and marsh surrounding this small lake that is part of the Niagara Escarpment World Biosphere Reserve near my home in southern Ontario. The lake is over ten thousand years old. Several years ago, scientists observed that the sediment in the lake was unlike that in many others: it has settled in the lakebed in undisturbed layers, allowing us to peer back in time across a thousand years.

The data found within these layers is believed to offer geological evidence for the Anthropocene, the proposed geological epoch in which human activity has left a globally consistent record in rock strata, documenting long-term changes to the earth system.[1] The proposed epoch would follow the Holocene, which started at the end of the last ice age roughly ten thousand years ago. Officially declaring a new geological era matters because it would also mean acknowledging that human activity has significantly changed Earth's natural systems.

Crawford Lake is the proposed "golden spike" site to mark the start of the Anthropocene, chosen out of many global candidates because its untouched sediment tells a clear story.[2] Core samples from the lake bottom display distinct annual layers from the last millennium. The layers show evidence of radioactive material from the development of nuclear technology in the 1950s. Earlier layers from the nineteenth century show records of the Crawford family's nearby sawmill, which milled lumber from trees felled by settlers as they cleared fields and expanded farmland across southern Ontario. Still earlier layers from the thirteenth to fifteenth centuries show records of corn pollen, grown by the inhabitants of a First Nations village, likely part of the Wendat Nation. This archaeological footprint is still visible at a site near the lake; a set of long-houses has been reconstructed on the original footprints. The Three Sisters Garden and Mashkiki Gitigan (Medicine Garden) located behind the longhouse village teach Indigenous agriculture techniques similar to what the original Wendat inhabitants may have practiced. I am contributing to the sediment of the lake as a present-day resident of southern Ontario; the fossil fuels that my car burned on the thirty-minute drive to Crawford Lake are part of the atmospheric particles that characterize the present moment in the story of humans and the earth. Someday, those particles, too, will end up on the bottom of the lake.

Defining the starting point of a new geological epoch is no easy decision. It is especially fraught when the stakes are high. There are political consequences to declaring when and how human activity has changed the planet enough to be considered a whole new epoch. Some scientists have proposed the beginnings of agriculture as the start date, and others propose the Industrial Revolution.[3] In the end, the researchers chose what is known as the Great Acceleration, a period starting in the 1950s when the impact of humans on the earth increased dramatically. This includes the development of nuclear technology as well as increasingly intensive practices for agriculture, mining, and fossil fuel extraction. In all, during the Great Acceleration, human production and consumption surpassed anything previously experienced in earth history.

While it is hard to argue with geologic records in sediment strata, the scientific debate illustrates the narrative power of crafting explanations and dating or defining ideas, in this case the Anthropocene. Where and how we start the story matters. It dictates what type of story we are telling. When we tell the story of the Anthropocene as a universal human issue linked to rapid global innovation and industrialization—one in which all human beings are equally to blame—it hides the disparities and injustices that led to our current climate and ecology. It also hides that the brunt of the resulting vulnerability is experienced unequally, falling most heavily on marginalized communities within North America and around the world.

French political scientist Françoise Vergès argues in a 2017 essay "Racial Capitalocene" that to understand the unevenly distributed impact of the climate and ecological crisis, we need to go back to the sixteenth century, to the unfolding of colonialism, empire-building, genocides, and the slave trade, and the economic system that arose from it all.[4] Our actions are never purely our own; we are always acting and reacting to what has come before us and the conditions around us that determine the available choices.

My family history is documented in the sediment at Crawford Lake. I'm a descendant of some of those early nineteenth-century European-origin settlers in southern Ontario who cut down trees and built roads, fences, and grain mills and laid the foundation for the British Empire's expansion at the expense of the Indigenous nations who have lived on this land for millennia. I grew up hearing stories of my ancestors as brave pioneers making a home in a new land where they could live in peace and practice their Anabaptist-Mennonite faith, itself a product of the sixteenth-century Reformation that pushed many religious minorities in Europe to seek new homes in

North America. Yet as I learn more about the history and present of this land where I live, the family story I want to tell my children is changing.

Stories shape culture. They tell us who and what is valued, and who and what is invisible or not worthy of note. Family origin stories can be especially powerful because they can tell us who we are and what our place in the world is. They create a sense of belonging and identity. They can ground us, helping us create meaning from the past and inspiring us through the stories of overcoming adversity to tackle obstacles in our lives. So what do you do when you realize that your family story, and the identity narrative that gave shape to your whole faith community, that led the shift from forest to field to pavement, is not the solid bedrock you thought it was? As I found, family and other ancestry stories can mislead us. Sometimes we have to relearn our history so we can tell it in new ways.

So much of what I knew of my family history was in the form of stories. To go deeper into their origins, I needed to find original documents and artifacts, see historical records, and piece together the stories I inherited into a larger context of what it means to be a descendant of early settlers in Ontario. I needed to start with research.

When I got to the university library reading room, the archivist brought out a heavy leather-bound tome and set it on a pillow, laying out a folder of newspaper clippings and yellow-edged letters in cursive on the tabletop beside the ancient book. Ensconced on this fluffy throne in front of me was nearly five hundred years of history.

It looks like it came from the Hogwarts library, I thought,
a bit embarrassed at my twenty-first-century pop culture gut
reaction. This was no movie prop from a children's fantasy
series. This was a Froschauer Bible, a Swiss German translation printed in Zurich, Switzerland, in 1531, in the midst
of the Reformation. The Reformation, which marked a profound shift in the practices and structure of the church, was
the launching point of Anabaptism, including my Mennonite
faith tradition. This Froschauer Bible was in my Reesor ancestors' possession when they arrived in what is now known as
Ontario in the early 1800s. Now it lives in the archives at
a university in Waterloo. For my Swiss Mennonite ancestors,
reading the Bible for themselves was a central pillar of the
heretical Anabaptist beliefs that got them exiled from their
home in Bern Canton, Switzerland. They then sought refuge
in Rhenish Bavaria (now Germany) before accepting William
Penn's offer of a life of religious freedom in the American colonies, and eventually moved north to Canada.

The archivist pointed out the missing straps, long since dis-
integrated. Though this book was made of paper, it was modeled after ancient parchment volumes that required straps to
keep parchment from morphing and bending with changes in
humidity. When released from their straps, these books would
sometimes spring open with coiled energy, spilling out their
pages into the light of day as if straining to unleash their ideas
into the world.

I felt that way about the heavy book in front of me. My
ancestors read this very Bible; it was the physical manifes-
tation of their Anabaptist belief in the importance of reading and interpreting Scripture together in the community of
believers and applying it to daily life. To avoid violence, to
tell the truth without needing oaths to bind your word, to let

adults choose to join the faith community through baptism, to seek simplicity, and to put conscience before loyalty to empire. Putting these ideas into practice had very real consequences; for my ancestors, to take these ideas seriously meant risking their homes, connections to family and community, and sometimes even their lives to state violence. Many early Anabaptists suffered martyrdom and death.

Looking closely at the pages, I could see spidery notes added to the margins that hinted at faithful study. The handwriting was tiny and faded, the old-fashioned script in a German dialect I don't know and couldn't see well enough to read even if I could understand it. Dates of births and weddings were inked onto the front and back covers. A page in the folder that accompanied the book translated some of the handwritten parts.

Sun. Apr. 8. 1808.
A daughter was born to us. This is Esther Reesor. Venus the ruling planet.

Other items in the archives from my Reesor ancestors include a deed from the early 1800s with affirmation that twelve acres of land in Markham was cleared of trees and fenced off. There's a necklace of amber beads for healing, and a booklet of recipes for curing various ailments, such as "Burkholders recipe (rye whiskey & lilly flowers)."

These records are their own layers in sediment, glimpses of a living past that undergirds our present just as rocks hold memories of ancient processes and environments that shape the terrain of the present. Processes can be gradual, like the receding Ice Age glaciers that shaped the land over millennia. Or they can be cataclysmic, like a meteorite cracking through the surface of the land, seeding new elements into the earth. The geology of southern Ontario, its distribution of rocks and the mineral and water resources within them, has influenced millennia of human settlement patterns.[5] These elemental resources allowed humans to thrive here, drew my own ancestors, and contribute to the growth of the City of Toronto and the surrounding towns and cities that spread outward each year as the pavement of urban sprawl consumes and destroys the soil and water resources that drew people to live here in the first place.

I'll tell you my family's story as I learned it growing up. But it is not true. Or at least, it's not the whole story. Like all family stories, the reality is messy and complicated. "To understand the past, we must investigate the stories we were not told, because those stories were withheld for a reason," writes activist Kelly Hayes in *Let This Radicalize You*. "We must search out all the pieces we weren't meant to find, the things that disrupt the narratives we've been given."[6] The deeper I go into the stories I've inherited, the more I realize that so many missing pieces were left out along the way.

I had thought my family history was a firm foundation, like the hard granite of the Canadian Shield rock formation that covers much of the province north of Toronto. Yet looking closer, I found flaking shale. There is no single story to be had. A simple narrative, tempting as it is, cannot capture the messy reality of the good and the bad all layered in together; particles of sand, shells, and pebbles—of action, intention, and memory—harden into the present land we stand on. It feels solid, yet it crumbles into fragments when you hold it in your hand for a closer look. I'm afraid that if I look too closely at these fragments, the layers of narrative and shared memory, I will lose more than a simple family heritage story. I'm afraid that the faith tradition I inherited alongside, and through, the stories handed down will turn out to be hollow.

The story as I learned it is a tale of persecuted religious minorities seeking peace and a simple kind of earthly flourishing. Moral and spiritual purity are the through lines, with family genealogy carefully traced back to original early Anabaptist forebears in Bern and Zurich. Along with the precious Froschauer Bible, my ancestors likely also owned a copy of *Martyrs Mirror*, an illustrated collection of stories about the religious martyrs of the Reformation and early Anabaptism. This text shaped many early Anabaptist understandings of who they were and where they came from. These are stories that reinforce the sense of my Swiss Mennonite ancestors being a people set apart, *in the world but not of the world* of British Upper Canada, and now the province of Ontario. "We are people of God's peace" begins a familiar hymn, its words drawn from the writings of sixteenth-century Dutch Anabaptist leader Menno Simons, whose followers became known as Mennonites. It's a song I've sung in church services and at peace rallies protesting wars. My spouse Luke and I included the song in our wedding service, a sung commitment to the kind of life that we want to lead together as people who live out a life of faith and service, to be the kind of people who repay harm with kindness and seek the good of all. With its ancient words, it is a song that connects me to the generations of Anabaptists, including those who were willing to die for their faith. When I hear it today, it has me wrestling with what it means to be a people of God's peace when that peace, I have come to find out, turns out to be built on a foundation of harm. I'm going back to the stories, the origin stories I learned, and looking at them with new eyes.

In 1796, at age twenty-one, my ancestor Peter Reesor rode his horse north from Pennsylvania through the dark evergreen forests of the Allegheny Mountains, forded the wide Susquehanna River and then the mighty Niagara, and so made his way by the shores of Lake Ontario to what is now the province of Ontario, sent by his Swiss Mennonite immigrant community in Pennsylvania to look for new opportunities for farmland and religious freedom.[7] He scouted land in what is now Waterloo Region, Ontario, deciding not to purchase land because of the complicated arrangement between the Six Nations, the British government, and an indebted land speculator. Though the land was the traditional territory of the Anishinaabe and Attawondaron Peoples as well as the Haudenosaunee, over a decade earlier, the British government of Upper Canada had granted to the Six Nations (Haudenosaunee Confederacy) ten kilometers of land on either side of the Grand River from its mouth at Lake Erie north to the river's head, for being allies of the British in the American War of Independence.[8] A land speculator named Richard Beasley purchased sections of this territory, known as the Haldimand Tract, from Six Nations, and then resold a portion of it, known as Block 2, to a group of Mennonite settlers from Pennsylvania. The funds from the land sales were intended to be held in trust for the "perpetual care and maintenance" of Six Nations of the Grand. Records show that the British-appointed trustees misappropriated the funds, and in many cases cannot account for where the monies went.[9]

In the family story I learned growing up, Peter Reesor stayed clear of Block 2 and headed elsewhere. He continued riding north and east of what is now Toronto, looking for black walnut trees, thought to indicate good soil. Near what is now the town of Markham, he traded his horse and saddle to purchase six hundred acres of land. As the story goes, he kept the bridle, as it wasn't part of the deal (thus demonstrating his thriftiness and good business sense) and walked all the way back to Pennsylvania with the bridle and the land title.

The land was empty, says the story, covered in thick forests that could be tamed to reveal the riches of agricultural production. My ancestors, with their generational European farming knowledge and deep-held beliefs in the value of hard work and simple living, were itching to take on the challenge of settling here, building their own promised land of religious freedom from the state and a life spent cultivating the bounty of the earth. They were pillars of a new settler community in the towns of Markham and Stouffville, people who kept family and faith at the center of it all.

I grew up on this land, on a farm between Markham and Stouffville that grows strawberries and sweet corn. Farming is my ancestral livelihood. I'm part of an unbroken line of farming families stretching back to pre-Reformation Europe. As a child, when I walked out past the windbreak line of trees sheltering the sunset-hued brick farmhouse, the faded red wooden barn, and the shop yard and felt the breeze pick up as I looked out on the long view of fields and gentle hills stretching into the distance, I felt that I belonged. I felt rooted to the land and to the community of Swiss Mennonite kinship. With the sun on my face and the smell of soil and growing things in my nose, I could imagine Peter striding across this land with a horse bridle looped over his arm, impatient to make the journey back to Pennsylvania.

"I found us a home!" he would tell his parents Fanny and Christian, back in Pennsylvania.

And it was a home. A good, good home for generations of their descendants. A good home for me.

Growing up, I accepted this founding story without question. Similar versions of this story are found all over my family tree: religious minorities seeking a peaceful agricultural existence fled Europe in the 1700s and settled across the eastern United States and Canada, living mainly in insular ethnoreligious communities where they farmed, worshiped in variations of German and English, fought over the adoption of new technology and appropriate apparel, and steadfastly resisted direct participation in war. My ancestors were people on the move for a long time. Switzerland to Germany, Germany to the American colonies, then north to Upper Canada. Born in Switzerland, died in Germany. Born in Friedelsheim, Germany, died in Elizabethtown, Pennsylvania; born in Elizabethtown, died in York County, Upper Canada. People on the move until this land, where they stayed and claimed it as home. Above all else, they did not doubt their presumed right to belong here, to settle on this land: to cut down trees, build roads, dam streams for mills, raise cattle, pigs, and chickens. Grow fields of oats and wheat to feed people and animals to sustain the rapidly growing population of the town of York, which became the city of Toronto. I loved this land too. I wanted to belong to it.

As I grew older, I spied cracks in this family heritage story that forced me to wrestle with my sense of identity. The first crack came in an endnote. Paging through a book on the history of Mennonites in Ontario, I read that the story of Peter trading his horse and saddle and walking back with the bridle couldn't have happened. While the family story celebrates 1804 as the year when Peter, Christian, Fanny, and family made the journey north by Conestoga wagon and began pioneer life in Markham, there's no written record of Peter or Christian Reesor owning land near Markham until 1805.[10] And certainly no records of purchasing the land years earlier, as the story of Peter and the bridle claims. So why tell the story at all? What was its purpose? And what else about the family narrative I'd heard my whole life might not be true? As I read accounts of Reesor family history and looked at historical records, the more confused I became. Dates were inconsistent from one account to the next. The story of heroic ancestors seemed more important than the facts.

The cracks in the story widened when I learned that Peter Reesor and his father Christian Reesor are listed as landowners on Block 2 of the Haldimand Tract, making them part of the group of Mennonite settlers who pooled their funds to purchase land from Six Nations through the land speculator Beasley in a transaction that remains contested to this day. I learned about my ancestors' history as early settlers only while studying the history of the community of Kitchener-Waterloo where I now live and own land. Centuries after the negotiation of the Haldimand Treaty, the Six Nations of the Grand River are still seeking an accounting of the money, property, and assets that were held in trust by the British Crown and its successors, the federal government of Canada and provincial government of Ontario, in an ongoing court case.[11] Though family lore said they hadn't, Peter and Christian had owned land on Block 2. Why didn't they stay? Historian Samuel J. Steiner notes that Peter's brother-in-law Abraham Stouffer is

documented as having a violent altercation with an Indigenous man while scouting land for a mill along the river near
Block 2. Steiner surmises that this may be what led Abraham
Stouffer and perhaps the rest of the Reesor family to settle in
Markham instead.[12] This story is not part of any family history
that I've heard orally or seen in family genealogy books. Why
wasn't this story handed down with the other stories? Was it
changed on purpose? Or not seen as important?

Another question arises: Why was the land in Markham
empty and available for purchase when my ancestors arrived?
Was it empty at all? I knew it had not always been so. Over the
years, plowing and discing up the fields would occasionally
turn up stone tools and pottery shards. First Nations had lived
here, farmed here. But where were they when my ancestors
arrived and started cutting down trees and building roads and
fences? Just gone. Not part of the story. As a student in public
school, I learned about Canadian history in general, including
the founding of Canada through confederation of the colonies
into provinces. But I learned nothing about the First Nations
living on the land where my schools were built or the land that
my family has called home for two hundred years.

I am learning now to say the names of those who have lived
on these lands over the millennia into the present: Wendat,
Attawondaron, Anishinaabe, Haudenosaunee. The history of
treaties and so-called land surrender is a living one; the land
my ancestors called empty is still the subject of outstanding
claims, including the Rouge River Valley Tract Claim lodged
in 2015 by the Mississaugas of the New Credit First Nation,
which includes the land where Peter Reesor cleared trees and
built grist mills on the Rouge.[13] And it covers the nearby land
of the farm where I grew up, now inside the boundaries of
Rouge Urban National Park.

I am beginning to learn, too, how the Indigenous nations that signed treaties understood these agreements much differently than the European nations they were engaged in treaty-making with. These insights change the stories I've been told. For example, the Anishinaabe Nation and the Haudenosaunee Confederacy established a formal relationship called "Our Dish," or the "Dish with One Spoon," related to the use of shared hunting grounds in the areas between the Great Lakes and the St. Lawrence river valley.[14] Anishinaabeg scholar Leanne Betasamosake Simpson writes that this precolonial agreement demonstrates a model for taking care of shared land while maintaining independence as sovereign nations. "It represented harmony and interconnection, as both parties were to be responsible for taking care of the dish."[15] Land is to be shared and jointly stewarded for the benefit of all living there, including the plant and animal nations who sustain life. Writing about the significance of early treaty-making processes to the Anishinaabe Nation, Simpson states that studying the processes of treaty-making between Indigenous nations matters because "these practices provide us with important insights into the kind of relationship our ancestors intended to have, and intended us to have with settler governments."[16]

My ancestors, citizens of settler-colonial Canada just as I am, were party to this expectation of shared stewardship and independence, though it seems to me that they did not know or understand it. But I know, and I am working to write this knowing into my family story and my faith story. My family's presence here on treaty lands, as treaty people ourselves in nation to nation relationships, is bound by responsibilities to the land and all those we share it with, both human and non-human life. I am learning that for those of us who are settlers and newcomers on this land, being part of the treaties is not about asserting our rights, but about honoring our responsibilities to care for, and to live in respectful ways with, all who live on this land, and to care for the land, too.

I am slowly getting a truer picture of my place, and the place of my ancestors in the larger community of people in Ontario. This land we now call southern Ontario was formed billions of years ago, shaped and regrown many times over; the time in which humans have existed here is the tiniest fraction of its history. The First Peoples arrived here as the Ice Age glaciers were receding, sculpting out and filling up the Great Lakes and their watersheds with meltwater. First Peoples have been continuously loving and caring for this land over eleven thousand years.[17] Pottery shards, scraping tools, stone tips for weapons, and other objects are layered in the strands of sediment across the province, carrying the imprint of hundreds of generations of Indigenous Peoples who have lived their lives, who have built societies and nations, who are nourished by and in turn nourish this land. Even as the ravages of settler-colonial power seek to erase Indigenous histories, languages, cultures, lives—genocide in every sense of the term—the rocks and soil, the layers of sediment, together with Indigenous Oral Traditions, bear witness to the long relationship between the people and land.

Even as I wrestle with my inherited legacy of harm and unjust privilege, I still see good seeds in my family and faith history. These are seeds of peace and justice, of enemy-love, of simple living as a virtue and the rejection of the hierarchies and titles of empire inside and outside of church walls, of a belief that when Jesus said "Blessed are the peacemakers," he was being serious. This is also part of what I have inherited. An essay in the Reesor family genealogy book traces our physical and spiritual ancestors back to 1400s Switzerland. It claims ancestors who were part of the Waldensian Christian movement, which valued simple living, the direct reading of Scripture, and the priesthood of all believers—values that probably supported them in later adopting an Anabaptist perspective at the risk of persecution and death. Just imagine, these seeds were planted more than five hundred years ago, longer ago even than that. And these seeds are still thriving today, growing and flourishing in new ways to meet changing contexts.

My family story, and the broader Swiss Mennonite community story—just one layer of the global Anabaptist movement—is full of people living their faith convictions. It is an important and compelling story of faith, one that continues to draw individuals and communities from many backgrounds beyond my specific ethnocultural community of ancestry into the larger Mennonite-Anabaptist faith community. Today, Mennonite churches and related Anabaptist groups in Canada are made up of many cultures and ethnicities. Mennonite World Conference, the body that connects the global community of Anabaptist and Mennonite church denominations, reports that nearly 85 percent of baptized believers in its member churches live in Africa, Asia, or Latin America, and just over 15 percent are in Europe and North America.[18]

Becoming conscientious objectors, missionaries, teachers, adoptive or foster parents—all of these are callings that my ancestors and community of faith have embraced in the project of being good and pure, of following God in word and deed. It is part of my life story, too, in my parents' choice to move our family from our Ontario farm to rural Haiti for a term of voluntary service. My parents were seeking to live out their faith-based peace convictions in response to the early 1990s Gulf War. I've also embraced these convictions and the influence of my faith heritage in my choices to pursue higher education in peace and conflict studies, political science, and community development, and then to be involved in social justice and community development work internationally and in Canada. To paraphrase Menno Simons, after whom the Mennonite faith tradition is named, true faith is not dormant but active in meeting the needs of the marginalized. The family story I inherited, that I live in my own life, is that we are people of faith and conviction who serve through growing food for others, through giving to charity, and through direct expressions of meeting tangible needs.

Ultimately, the founding story of my family is one of being good, of doing good. Of being spiritually pure in lived ways, like refusing to swear oaths (we affirm—never swear—when called on to be in court). Refusing military service. Building institutions dedicated to resettling refugees, feeding hungry people with crops and with donations, helping—always helping. We were persecuted for our faith, but we stayed faithful at great personal cost.

Pulling at this thread of goodness, this historic through line of family narrative, threatens to unravel my identity as well as my family's carefully constructed centuries-old identity. Is that what makes retelling this story so difficult? Piecing together the shifting dates and ballooning narrative feels like dragging a plow through dry, packed soil. It is hard because I have been born, raised, conditioned, to be good at all costs. To do good, to be good. *Be perfect as your heavenly Father is perfect.* Is my history worthless or categorically bad if it is not perfect? If it is not uncorrupted and pure?

I am now learning, we are learning, about how the narrative of goodness and purity itself has perpetuated harm. How can I find my way from trying to be good to trying to be a good neighbor? Not seeking to "be" morally pure, but seeking to live in harmony and with respect for people and the natural world that sustains all life. As Black feminist political theorist and abolition activist Robyn Maynard describes it: "To value collective livingness, to touch and know life fully, to know a life that is not in some way predicated on and subsidized by the suffering of another: I suspect that this is what liberation is."[19]

I am coming to know, to see and name, what has been unspoken in my history: that my life has been predicated on and subsidized by the suffering of others. It's a painful self-reckoning, because so much of my identity and family story has been based on a myth of goodness and morality. For those like me who come from dominating cultures and ethnic groups, how do we set down the need to be "good" and move into a new way of understanding ourselves as humans, as people in systems who have participated in harmful and beneficial ways? As people who can have the emotional fortitude to seek out and sit with the truth, hard as it is, to more clearly understand where we fit into all of this and what the next steps of action and reconciliation look like. What repair looks like. We have to be strong enough to understand ourselves as having caused harm, humble enough to live with the shame of that burden, and courageous enough to have the persistence and commitment to learn more, to do better, and to work for repair. It is difficult work, yes, but it is freeing work, too.

I'm striving to learn how to honor my own elders and those who have gone before me when that history is also wrapped up in layers of harm. How can I acknowledge it all, and then choose what to take and what to leave behind? I'm picking through the fragments, looking for what I want to celebrate in my culture and heritage, and what I acknowledge as part of my history but choose to leave behind me. It is more than a lifetime's work. And it is shame work: the work of coming to terms with unearned privilege and knowledge of how my ancestors knowingly and unknowingly caused harm and devastation to Indigenous and Black communities—sometimes directly and sometimes through inaction. Tempting as it is sometimes, I can't just throw it all out and start fresh. The past comes with us, and it's a gift to know it. It is a form of privilege, of power, to know my family history at all, and to have preserved records that give insight into the past. This is in contrast to the forced erasure of the past for Indigenous Peoples through genocide, residential schools, and adoptions, and through the violence of the trans-Atlantic slave trade. It is a privilege to have detailed records of my ancestors.

For my mostly White ancestors and relatives, engaging with the truth is a choice. Privilege allows us to look away, to choose when and how to engage. But sediment doesn't lie. The record in rocks keeps track. At Crawford Lake, the geological record of human impact on the planet is marked in layers of sediment. The historical and institutional records show a clear chronicle of harm, including incarceration rates, land ownership rates, health outcomes, child welfare statistics . . .

I'm continually getting lost on this journey of reclamation, stumbling in the marshlands of guilt and apathy. How easy to label the past as tainted, corrupted, and to throw it away. For those like me from settler-dominant backgrounds, we need to do the careful work of analyzing layers and components, of being mindful of the pressures and forces acting on the individuals making choices. Because hard and true elements run through it all that are worth finding and preserving. The more we learn, build relationships with others and expand our worldviews, the richer the experience of living in a geographic place. It is like holding up a grey stone to sunlight and seeing the glitter of crystal and veins of color glow.

As I see more and more of the richness and complexity of what it means to live in treaty together on Turtle Island, I can't help but seek out more knowledge. It is painful to recognize the delusion of my initial understanding of what it means to live here, of what it means to be a descendant of settlers. To inherit a religious tradition that perpetuated cultural genocide against Indigenous Peoples, and through citizenship to be party to agreements between nations including the Haldiman Treaty that covers the land where I live. That is why I keep showing up to learn and to do things differently than my physical and spiritual ancestors. I find the work of relearning my history exhausting and uncomfortable. There are no clear hallmarks or objectives. It is a process of committing again and again to keep showing up to the work of learning and unlearning. And it is a sign of my privilege that I always have the option of pulling back, pulling away, choosing comfort and safety. But I don't want to live a lie.

My hope for all of us is to live in relationships of mutuality, understanding our interconnection with the social and economic systems that we are embedded in and how that affects our local and global neighbors and the natural world of which we humans are a part. As in Robyn Maynard's definition of liberation, we need to keep examining the layers of our history and our present to know where our existence has come, and comes, at the cost of others' suffering so that we can work toward freeing ourselves from causing harm. So that we can work toward repair.

This is the evolving story that I tell my children when I talk about our history. As I learn more, I change it and add details, looking for authenticity above all else. Our ancestors came to what is now called southern Ontario looking to build the kind of life they valued, centered around family, faith, simple living, and the hard work of growing food to feed cities. They had degrees of power and privilege and became part of the colonial system that caused harm. Their prosperity came at the cost of others' suffering. Now we know, I tell my children, and we need to learn from this, too, to understand our obligations to live well with people and land, and to seek justice. Our values of faith and family heritage are resources that help us live into these obligations so that we, and our neighbors locally and globally, and the natural world that we are a part of, too, can live in harmony together.

I remind my children that one of the most important aspects of our Mennonite-Anabaptist faith tradition is that faith is lived in practical ways, in actions and choices made every day. We are learning, we are gaining new understanding, we are paying attention to seen and unseen impacts all around us. By paying attention to cultures and systems that we participate in, by examining how we live in community together, and by practicing the skills and habits of accountability and repair, we have the chance to do things differently. To live a different kind of future together as neighbors and relations.

Memory and history, the layers and fragments of experience and story handed down to us, are a resource we can tap into to find our way forward together as people who live in community, in society, in our diversity. Poet and essayist Dionne Brand writes about the struggle to define a Canadian identity that is not dominated by the colonial imagination of the English and French cultures that shaped the nation-state named Canada. She calls us to question and resist the myth of a homogeneous Canadian culture. There must be space for multiple stories, for "buried and new visions other than those of the dominating culture."[20] In some cases the memories and stories we draw on give us insight and courage into how to navigate challenging times. I still sing the songs, the old hymns, that have sustained my ancestors, drawing strength and leaning into the four-part harmony of voices that carries my voice along too. Songs sung through births and deaths, fall bounty and failed harvests. And in some cases the memories and stories give me the teachings I need, the wisdom to say "Never again" to actions that dehumanize, exploit, erase.

It is a tradition in Canada to wear red velvet poppy pins on November 11, marked as Remembrance Day in honor of the armistice to the First World War. Throughout Canada, students wear the pins at assemblies, where they recite poems about poppies blowing in the wind on Europe's battlefields and graveyards. The red button I wear instead of a poppy says "To Remember Is to Work for Peace." This button movement started over twenty years ago as a way to link the memory of the horrors of war with the need for ongoing peace work today. Some choose to wear their buttons side-by-side with a poppy, honoring the memory of fallen soldiers and seeking to imagine a different way forward. The phrase "To remember is to work for peace" calls us to remember the horrors of the First and Second World Wars, the devastation wrought on civilians and soldiers across Europe, North America, and other parts of the world. It means we must remember history so that we can avoid the horrors and bloodshed of warfare as we move forward. It is a call to governments to consider true pathways to peace, not the doomed cycle of armed violence.

Yet I think it is time to also wear my red button as a memento of my own family history; to wear it as a token of remembrance of my inheritance of harm as the descendant of early settlers and as a spiritual inheritor of a faith tradition that believed Indigenous cultures and traditions were less valuable than its own. I cannot ignore that history. It has shaped me, shaped my family, shaped my worldview and sense of belonging in the world for good and ill, as it has shaped the lives and lived experiences of others. To deny it is to pretend that it doesn't matter, but it does. The past comes with us, and it is up to us to decide how to tell the stories, what meaning to ascribe them, how to unpack the power and privilege, and the vulnerabilities, that we inherit from our ancestors. To remember is to work for peace, for justice, for reconciliation. It is to listen to and tell many stories and not a single dominant one that obscures all others.

From earth history to human history, the stories we tell shape possible futures. The history of the Anthropocene is a story of what happens when the exploitation of people and the exploitation of the environment are connected. The history of this land where I live is a story that includes Indigenous treaty-making between nations and between humans and the plant and animal nations, treaties that supported good, sustainable relationships between peoples and between peoples and the natural world. I am learning this history and working to make it part of our new family story as residents on this land. This is the work we are all called to do, in our corners of this earth—courageously looking at the stories we've inherited, the stories we tell about ourselves and our place in the world, and being willing to question them for a truer picture of what it means to live in relationship with people and the natural world around us. Owning this responsibility means looking back at the stories we've inherited, that have provided meaning in our life, and evaluating whether they serve the goal of a future where everyone, people and the natural world, can thrive.

In *Braiding Sweetgrass*, a book that considers Indigenous wisdom, scientific insights, and lessons from the natural world, scientist and Potawatomi citizen Robin Wall Kimmerer calls us to choose a story of reciprocity and gratitude. A story in which we understand the natural world not as a set of commodities to be produced, bought, and sold, clear-cut and fenced off, but as a common resource in a reciprocal relationship of gifts. "The moral covenant of reciprocity calls us to honor our responsibilities for all we have been given, for all that we have taken," she writes. "It's our turn now, long overdue."[21]

Responsibility, reciprocity, gratitude, and mutual flourishing. These values offer us a foundation for courageous change. That's a story of people and the earth that I want to be part of writing into the geological record, setting the foundation for a flourishing future.

3

RETELLING CREATION STORIES

For my family, as for many urban dwellers around the world, seeing the stars has become a rare treat, one that must be planned and scheduled. Streetlights and the luminary debris of our electrified cities and towns, along with smog and haze in the atmosphere, are changing our relationship to the night sky. On our changing planet, seeing the constellations is transforming from a common night-time occurrence to something that is mythical as much as tangible.

One evening when our son was three, Luke and I realized that Isaac had no memory of ever seeing stars. We read him books about space, and he was curious about planets and the sun and black holes. But from our city home, we rarely saw more than a pinprick. It was an Ontario winter evening, already fully dark by six o'clock. Luke and I made the last-minute decision to bundle Isaac and our newborn daughter Ava into the car and drive twenty minutes from our house downtown into the countryside. Away from the veil of city lights, we pulled over into the empty parking lot of a farm machinery workshop. Stamping our feet against the cold, we watched our breath condense into clouds around us. We stargazed until the frigid air sent us scrambling for the car's warmth.

A few years later when we were on vacation at a lake in northern Ontario, I woke up six-year-old Isaac at ten thirty. We walked out to the dock for a view of the night sky, expansive and filled with stars. I pointed out the Big Dipper and Orion, the only two constellations I can identify by sight. Passing on the knowledge of just those two shapes in the sky seemed important, a key part of life knowledge and historical record, part of the family story of being human in the vast universe that I wanted him to know too. The story of people looking up at constellations that hold both great mystery and a familiar map of human belonging in the universe. Nothing keeps us humble like looking at the stars and contemplating the immensity of the universe and our limited human existence in a fragment of time and space.

Stars have been a more constant companion in human history than almost anything else in our ever-changing earthly home. Stars are keepers of stories, keepers of maps. Stars have sparked wonder and curiosity throughout humanity's lifetime—some cave walls contain thirty-thousand-year-old paintings of stars. Stars have pointed to freedom, pointed to home; they point us to our seeming insignificance in the expanse of time and space in the universe. Stars, we now know, formed elements in our bodies and provide the building blocks needed to sustain life in our world.[1]

And we know that the light we see today is a relic from the past; the time it takes to cover the distance between the stars and our eyes means that we are watching distant history. The Andromeda Galaxy, the furthest thing we can see with unassisted eyes in the night sky, is 2.5 million light-years away. The starlight we see today was cast before humans appeared.

Like learning about geology, studying the stars is a humbling reminder of the tiny window of time in which humans as a species have been part of the unfolding story of creation.

The night sky is both constant, in its long timelines and slow changes, and evolving, with stars being born and collapsing into black holes. Evolving, too, is humanity's knowledge of stars and space. Our understanding of the universe is growing in leaps and bounds as advancing technology and new discoveries in cosmology expand what we know and raise more questions about what we don't. Scientists now estimate that everything we can see and experience in the universe—all the so-called normal matter of plants and people and rocks and stars and gas and the elements—makes up only 5 percent of the universe.[2] The rest is dark energy and dark matter—*dark* because it is not visible in the way that normal matter is. Scientists know it exists because they can observe its effects, but they can't observe it directly. We still know more about what this dark energy and dark matter is not than what it definitively is. As I learn more about the origins of the universe and the potential end of the universe on its trajectory of acceleration and expansion, I am awestruck by how rare life is, and thus how sacred all forms of life are.

My grandma Anna, at ninety-nine years old, can still recite a poem she learned as a schoolgirl.

> Great, wide, beautiful, wonderful World,
> With the wonderful water round you curled,
> And the wonderful grass upon your breast—

World, you are beautifully drest [*sic*] . . .

The poem rhapsodizes further about the beauty of the world, and after several verses, it concludes:

Ah, you are so great, and I am so small,
I tremble to think of you, World, at all;
And yet, when I said my prayers to-day,
A whisper inside me seemed to say,
"You are more than the Earth, though you are such a dot:
You can love and think, and the Earth cannot!"[3]

It's a lovely poem, full of wonder and gratitude. Yet I've grown uncomfortable with the last line. Am I really more than the earth? And *can* the nonhuman Earth love? Or think? Can being human ever be untangled from being earthly? The more I learn about science and the natural world and our embeddedness in it as human creatures, the more I realize just how much the human/nature divide breaks down. My story of being human in the universe is changing.

In my early teen years, my favorite series of books, my favorite world to inhabit, was Madeline L'Engle's science fiction classic *A Wrinkle in Time* and the four books that followed it. Galaxies and quarks, mitochondria, and time-space tesseracts are the backdrop to a cosmic struggle between good and evil. L'Engle's writing is filled with wonder, reverence, and awe, inspiring a contagious curiosity that has stuck with me and a belief that the actions of individuals for good or ill matter in the universe. L'Engle's Time Quintet inspired me to keep learning about the micro and macro worlds that are part of our existence even though they are beyond our day-to-day observation.

In exploring the miracles and mysteries of the universe, I feel a profound connection with God's divine force of love and life. My sense of awe and spirituality is heightened. Whether contemplating what it means to be human or the blurry boundaries and spaces between the particles and electrons that make up what we perceive as matter, our existence is best understood in relationship to our kin in creation. To sit on the granite slope of a northern Ontario lakeshore on a clear summer night and watch stars appear, to know that those stars reflected in the still mirror of water at my feet are images from ancient history, to know that the matter of our bodies, made of roughly thirty trillion cells,[4] are formed with elements that originated in the furnace of stars . . . to know these things, and to know that there so much we don't yet know and will never know about the intricate jigsaw of the universe, is a humbling and spiritual experience. By spiritual, I mean that the awe I feel is linked to mystery, to the unknowable, to faith in a Creator who is beyond my human powers of observation and comprehension.

What does it mean for human beings to be thinking, loving, creative beings, made in the image of our Creator, amid this vast, unknowable, interconnected universe? Our understanding of ourselves, the stories we tell ourselves about ourselves—in this universe, and the world shaped by our human actions—have the power to lead us toward a culture of interconnected, reciprocal flourishing for people and the natural world. Alternatively, our creation stories can drive us further down the path of exploitation and harm to both people and the natural world, not only on our planet but beyond. As we strive for a healthier future, does it matter whether we think of ourselves as having more intrinsic worth than the earth or whether we take a humbler approach? I think it does.

How did my ancestors come to think that they were entitled to clear-cut forests and dam streams for mills? Why do politicians and land developers today think it is okay to remove the environmental protections that were established to safeguard those same fields and remaining wetlands? As someone living in a modern-day Canadian city, many of my day-to-day actions also follow this logic: driving a car with fossil fuel, using a phone with a battery made of minerals mined in environmentally and socially damaging ways. It feels impossible to disentangle myself from a society where my daily actions are presupposed on exploiting natural resources and the labor of people in other parts of the world.

As I try to pay attention to the daily ethics of my urban Canadian lifestyle, the more I realize its fundamental assumptions about people being the most important thing on Earth. As a person from a privileged, White middle-class background, I've also come to realize that my lifestyle includes baked-in assumptions about what I should be able to access and consume cheaply and comfortably without regard for what and who makes that consumption possible. The status quo of overconsumption and inequality cannot continue if we're going to shift the direction of life on our planet toward a better future for all.

The stories we tell about the creation of the earth and of human beings shape our thinking about entitlement and who has the right to consume. In an influential 1967 essay about the roots of our ecological crisis, the historian Lynn White draws links between Western, Judeo-Christian beliefs about creation and the role of human beings. White contends that the dominant Western worldview got us into this global climate and ecological crisis. Believing that nature exists solely for the benefit of people has led to the unsustainable use of natural resources, including fossil fuels. "What people do about their ecology depends on what they think about themselves in relation to things around them," writes White. "Human ecology is deeply conditioned by beliefs about our nature and destiny—that is, by religion."[5]

Like White, ecofeminist theologian Rosemary Radford Ruether has also examined the beliefs undergirding the current dominant patterns of consumption and extraction. Ruether sees creation stories as blueprints for society.[6] They are bundles of assumptions about knowledge, about relationships between humans and the natural world. That is, assumptions about how things should be, how they ought to be. Creation stories are both reflections of worldviews and a way to pass along those worldviews to future generations. Ruether also calls attention to the fingerprints of Western European Christian thought on the patterns of beliefs and actions that have justified overextraction of natural resources and destruction of the environment for human purposes. She contends that exploitation of the natural world is interconnected with oppression and domination of some people over other people, manifesting in racism, colonization, and sexism. We can trace this back to Western Christian interpretations of the creation story in Genesis, which placed humans over all else in nature and modeled hierarchies replicated throughout the social structure. Human over nature, men over women, royalty over peasants, people of European ancestry over all other people. The story of hierarchy, of so-called divinely mandated entitlement by some to consume, leached into our world's social and economic systems.

In the face of the rising challenges of the global climate and environmental crisis, technology is often held up as the key to solving all problems. But new technology won't change the harmful relationships among people and between people and the natural world. Values, our beliefs about the world and our place in it, and our origin stories are part of the social blueprint of our world. Addressing the climate crisis and the time of ecological devastation that we are in requires a deeper culture shift. Just as with our ancestry stories, we need to examine what we've inherited and to consider different stories, and different interpretations of known stories, to shape a healthier future.

As a descendant of European settlers and an inheritor of the Western stream of Christianity, I think it is important to find ways to tell a different story about the place of humans in the cosmos, one in which people are interconnected in creation—part of it, but not the center. I want to tell a different creation story, one with a different bundle of assumptions and ethical mandates that lean toward flourishing not just for some, but for all. This will help me plant and tend seeds for flourishing as I learn how to think beyond the hierarchy and binaries of the old story to embrace a better story of embodied interdependence and mutuality.

I can picture my Reesor ancestors reading from the book of Genesis in their sixteenth-century leather-bound family Bible, the familiar narrative shaping their understanding of creation and the role of human beings in the world. The hand-colored woodcut illustrations of the garden where Adam and Eve's lushly rounded bodies lounge in verdant splendor inspiring their imaginations. Day and night, water and land, good and evil, dominion and natural order. God who brings life and creates order out of chaos. God the namer, the gardener, the farmer, who created and provided the bounty of the earth for the benefit of human beings, who were then responsible for stewarding this bounty and using it well.

As with other European-origin Christians at the time, my ancestors' understanding of this creation story centered on the idea that humans reflect the divine image of God on Earth; men are divinely created leaders and women are their helpers and comforters. And, as the Catholic Church leaders and the European royalty set out in papal bulls justifying their empire-building atrocities, European Christians were the most divinely appointed of all. Only European Christians, they claimed, fully counted as human beings, and any land not ruled by European Christians should be considered empty and ripe for conquest. This spiritual violence, known as the Doctrine of Discovery, shaped the world as we know it today, paving the way for the trans-Atlantic slave trade and the physical and cultural genocide against Indigenous Peoples around the world.

This theology of human dominance can still be found in conservative evangelical theology. One such example is theologian Wayne Grudem's influential book *Systematic Theology*, still a primary teaching text for many conservative Christian seminaries and Bible colleges. In Grudem's view, human beings are the "pinnacle of God's creation" and are "appointed to rule over the rest of creation." Grudem argues that understanding the nature of creation as fundamentally good means that humans should enjoy and use earthly resources for their own and other humans' benefit. Grudem's emphasis on the fleeting, temporary nature of creation in comparison to the eternalness of God diminishes any responsibility to care for and protect the natural world. The earth and its bounty are for humans in the current age and have no significance in God's eternal, heavenly kingdom.[7] All of this will pass away. And it *will* pass away, one way or another, according to astrophysicists like Katie Mack, whose 2020 popular science book *The End of Everything* details five theories—based on quantum mechanics, string theory, and cosmology—of what will happen on the other end of the Big Bang that birthed the universe.

But what happens in between? What happens for generation after generation of human beings living in a world that previous generations have seen fit to consume and destroy without thought of those who come afterward? Centuries after the Industrial Revolution and the trans-Atlantic slave trade, the harms past and present to Indigenous communities in North America and to nations in the Global South persist. Mining destroys sacred landscapes, and chemicals and heavy metals like mercury leak into waterways and ecosystems with devastating effects for generations. All of this occurs so that people mainly like me, with my European ancestry and North American middle-class lifestyle, can live in comfort, content to believe that God's creation is good and exists solely for our immediate benefit.

We know that we need to radically re-vision daily habits and patterns of interaction. Things cannot continue as they are. It would take more than five Earths to support the average Canadian and American lifestyle for all human beings, and we have only one planet to call home.[8] But it is hard to make these changes alone. This is where faith communities, including churches, can be transformative in the climate crisis, embodying new cultural values that enable the society-wide changes necessary to move away from a value system of hierarchy, domination, and extraction to value systems centered on the interdependent thriving of all. We can get there only by looking closely at the beliefs that currently shape our actions individually and as communities. The challenge is worth wrestling with: How do we tell the story of human beings differently, one not of hierarchy but interdependence?

The stories we tell are tied to the languages we speak, the words available to us to give meaning to what we perceive around us. The languages we speak also contain assumptions, ethics, and values that construct and support our worldviews. Julian Guamán, an Indigenous Mennonite author and church leader from the Ecuadorian Andes, described the significant difference in worldview that he experienced in learning Spanish compared to his first language of Kichwa, which can be traced back to the Incas. He contends that the structure of Spanish, the language of the colonizers who defeated the Inca Empire and controlled most of South America in the 1500s, lends itself to objectification and thus exploitation of the natural world:

> If human beings have a worldview that puts them outside of . . . the environment, they are able to objectify a tree, an animal, a bird . . . (even more so) the minerals, the rocks, the river, the water, the air. . . . They see them as objects: as tradable, as negotiable, as sellable, as buyable, as manipulatable, as controllable.
>
> In contrast, Kichwa relies less on nouns and more on verbs, expressing interactions and interconnections more than actions done by someone to something. As Guamán explained, "This forms the foundation for the Andean worldview that is based in parity, in relationship, in coexistence, in interaction, in harmony, in equilibrium."[9]

In *Braiding Sweetgrass*, Robin Wall Kimmerer makes a similar observation, comparing Potawatomi, an Anishinaabe language, to English. She uses the phrase "the grammar of animacy" to describe the structure of the language, which conveys that the natural world is alive in the same way that people are alive. By contrast, English relies heavily on nouns and objects that are acted on, as opposed to living beings that exist in their own right.[10] In another essay, Kimmerer observes that while there is no perfect correlation between the animacy of a language and the actions of its speakers (as she notes, she grew up speaking English and has yet to clear-cut a forest), language shapes how we think and feel about what is around us. "English encodes human exceptionalism," writes Kimmerer, "which privileges the needs and wants of humans above all others and understands us as detached from the commonwealth of life."[11]

I am not a linguist or a speaker of Kichwa or Potawatomi, and I am in no position to compare their grammatical structures. But as a native English speaker and writer, I am coming to see how my first language is constructed very differently from these languages, as described by Kimmerer and Guamán. I can see that a language has implications for culture in terms of what concepts can be expressed, and how, in daily life and conversations. In English, for example, we refer to animals as "it" unless we have a relationship with them, in which case we use personal pronouns. The stray dog is an "it," the pet a "good girl." In a small step toward a more relational understanding of the world around me, I am learning the names of the plants, grasses, and herbs in my yard. To know that the plant I'm digging out of the strawberry patch is not just a nameless weed, but a plant sometimes called broadleaf plantain, and that like me it is also a descendant of colonization and is now part of the ecosystem in my community for better and for worse. I am trying to shift how I use language to transform the way I see myself in the world, and thus change how I act, shifting toward interdependence.

To exist is to be in community, to be in reciprocal relationship with people and with the natural world, explained Guamán. He described this focus on community and interdependence, along with the mandate to care for the environment as well as for people, as a place of overlap of the Kichwa culture he grew up in and the Mennonite beliefs and practices that shape his faith and witness. For him, to understand oneself as having a responsibility to other people and to the natural world, to live in community, and to practice reconciliation—making things right and bringing relationships into harmony again—is a practice of lived discipleship, of following Jesus and a way of life that has tangible implications. The lands controlled by Indigenous Peoples in the Andes have been more protected from extractive and exploitative mining practices than other parts of Latin America. Guamán attributed this to the Kichwa worldview that sees people's relationships with places as sacred. Protecting and preserving place is part of living *ayni*, or interdependence. Thus, protecting land from exploitation is also a form of lived discipleship.[12]

Guamán's words speak to the longing in my soul for a way of living, a faith tradition, that brings together the sacred and the everyday. Interdependence, community, mutual flourishing, reconciliation—these values resonate with the beliefs I've learned from my Anabaptist-Mennonite ancestors, and they give me hope for living out a different story of belonging and interdependence in the community of the cosmos. Learning theology from faith leaders who are Indigenous and Mennonite in Ecuador is the bridge I've been looking for to bring a new lens, a new way of telling the story of creation that will move from human domination to mutual flourishing. Through hearing diverse perspectives on interpreting the Christian creation story, I see the possibility of earthly redemption, of renewal, a path toward reconciliation with people and with the earth itself, this interconnected, amazing, unique host of life in our vast universe. It is a journey of listening, of encountering, of looking with new eyes. It pushes me to keep seeking perspectives that stretch my understanding.

The creation theology that I grew up with was one of stewardship: people are entrusted by God to manage and use well the gifts of earthly abundance. As I seek to deepen my understandings of responsibility, mutuality, and interconnection with others and with the natural world, the role of humans as separate from other parts of creation feels increasingly uncomfortable. In expressing a relationship of mutuality between humans and the natural world, I'm drawn to the thinking of theologian Randy Woodley, a Cherokee descendant who writes about being part of the community of creation, which seeks restoration of harmony between not just people but also "the Creator, the earth, and all that God provides through the earth such as plants and animals."[13] The understanding of shalom as a community of creation challenges the usual Christian environmental perspective which places humans in a distinct and higher role over the rest of creation. If I believe that we have a duty to live in harmony with all creation rather than a stewardship duty to care for all creation, how might I think or act differently? The call to "live in harmony" with all creation opens up a path of mutuality and interdependence.

Theologian Austen Hartke found that as he grew to understand and embrace his transgender identity, he grew in understanding the complexities within the binary categories in the Genesis creation story. "Biologically, I learned that the world isn't separated distinctly into land or sea; there are also marshes, estuaries, and coral reefs," Hartke writes. There is dusk within the separation of light and darkness, and complex ecosystems at the meeting points of water and dry land. There is diversity and complexity in the space between gender and sex binaries of male and female. This extends to how we as humans fit in complex and interconnected ways within the infinite diversity of life in the universe. The divide between human beings and the rest of life in the cosmos becomes less important than what may exist in the space between. As Hartke writes, "Instead of asking the text to define and label all that is, we can ask God to speak into the space between the words, between biblical times and our time, and between categories we see as opposites."[14] It's an embrace of complexity and interconnection that builds on the poetic categories of land and sea, light and dark, human and animal, but is not limited by them.

Now when I read the creation stories in Genesis 1 and 2, I imagine the creator of mist and mountains, of broadleaf plantain and sea pigs, cultivating an emerging community of relationships. Psalm 104 captures this vision, describing a God who provides for animals and birds and people without distinction, the creator of the universe who cares about the well-being of each creature in it.

If we humans know anything about life in the universe, it is that it is precious and seemingly rare. According to astrobiologist Kevin Peter Hand of NASA's Jet Propulsion Laboratory, we just don't know what life on other planets might look like, if it does exist. All we know is that so far, the only living things found in the universe are on Earth—but theoretically, the conditions for life could arise or be present on other planets or moons. In the Milky Way Galaxy alone, there could be billions of planets with Earth-like conditions. Even so, extremely rare circumstances led to the emergence of life on Earth. We really may be alone in the universe as a species exploring the stars. We don't know either way. Hand states:

> It could be that life and the origin of life is a singularity. It's only occurred here on Earth. And we are the first and only instance of it. And so if we do go out and explore and we don't find life elsewhere, that also is pretty profound because that means that life is rare. And it also puts an even bigger onus on us to take care of the only life we know.[15]

As we study the possibility of life on other planets and imagine language evolving to one day communicate with an extraterrestrial lifeform, what about unidentified languages on our own planet? What if we were to discover that trees and fungi and animals and insects and coral reefs are all talking, if we would only listen? The more that scientists develop techniques to ideate communication and language in imagined others somewhere out there in the vastness of the universe, the more we may realize that life on our planet is communicating and we humans are not as alone on our planet as we believed. We are surrounded by our kin and learning to hear their voices in new ways.

In recent years, orca whales, a critically endangered species, have attacked and even sunk boats off the coast of Spain and Portugal. We don't know why.[16] Is it a new fad? Something the whales are just weirdly into? Or is it a coordinated response to a history of harmful encounters with boats? Maybe the whales are trying to perform a play of Psalm 104:26, which references the sea monster Leviathan frolicking around ships. Whatever the reason, it's perfect fodder for snarky social media comments about whales taking responsibility to protect ocean life when human governments are failing at it. Scientists don't have a clear-cut explanation for the behavior. We don't know what the orcas are trying to say with their actions. It continues to muddy the water around what sentience and intelligence in the natural world really means.

Recent research on fungi also raises questions about non-human communication. Scientists have identified repeated patterns of electrical pulses, similar in length to human words, transmitted through the long, threadlike mycelium network that connects mushrooms underground.[17] Analyzing the signal length, and the repeated patterns of spiking signals, scientists found what may be a lexicon of about forty "words" used by fungi to share information. What do mushrooms talk about? Tree gossip? Beetle parties? The sacred cycle of life, death, decomposition, and renewal? We don't know. But it changes my view of what it means for the fungi I see clinging to fallen logs or popping up after a rainfall to be alive, to be intelligent. It pushes me to find a way to bring the worldview of Kimmerer's "grammar of animacy," as well as the Kichwa, into my daily English-language existence to better reflect my shifting understanding of the dynamic nature of the world, of the cosmos.

It's new for me to read Scripture with a focus on the non-human description. I was raised to read the Bible with a social justice lens, one focused on transforming oppression of the poor and excluded, of reconciling and restoring relationships between people and between people and the divine. But when I go back through the sacred stories and Psalms with this new lens of interconnection, I find a Bible full of images of the natural world communicating in dynamic ways. Rocks that cry out, trees clapping their hands, the heavens declaring God's glory, a burning bush housing God's divine presence. The world as described in the Bible is in conversant flow, interconnected between human, natura, and divine. In the Genesis 2 creation account, the first human being is shaped from the earth itself, formed out of the same soil that is later planted into a garden, the garden of Eden. We are earthly creatures, as divinely evolved in our own way as every other living being (terrestrial and extraterrestrial) and every form of matter (and dark matter, and antimatter, and the kinds of matter we don't know about yet).

To move forward with courageous change toward a reconciled, interconnected, flourishing, livable future for all, including nonhuman life, we must tell a different story, one of finding meaning in our dependency—not domination—on the natural world of which we are a part. By pulling these threads together—of Indigenous ways of understanding interconnection, of queer theology's understanding of the richness and intricacy of the space between binary categories, of my own awakening to the limitations of the creation story I inherited—I work to weave a different story, one that will fill the spaces of my life, my community, and the beliefs I pass on to my children and future generations.

The story I will tell my son Isaac, and my daughter Ava as she gets older, about what it means to be human will be a story that puts us in the middle of creation. Not middle as in center, but middle as in surrounded and embraced on all sides. We'll sit on the glacier-formed granite slopes of a backcountry campsite in northern Ontario, part of our family tradition of summer canoe out-tripping. It will be late at night—at least ten o'clock, maybe eleven if they can stay awake that long after bedtime—as we wait for the daylight to dissolve into the black canvas of night sky. We'll hear the faint siren of a mosquito, kept at bay by the breeze off the lake, and listen to the occasional sound of water shimmering as a fish surfaces or a muskrat slips into the lake.

Remember this, I will say, as we lean back on the cool stone ledge beneath us to see the stars emerging in their multitudes. Remember that you are a miraculous creation of earth and stardust amid a universe of miraculous creations, and that you are no more miraculous than any other. We have a duty to care for this world, to live in harmony in ways that allow others, human and beyond, to flourish too. And it is by living together well that all of us thrive together. How amazing, I will tell them, how amazing to be not the center of this universe, but an interconnected element in it, living in joy and gratitude for the divine goodness that sustains our shared life on this planet.

RENEWING

4

RENEWING OUR HOPE AND TRANSFORMING DESPAIR

A friend who is in his seventies recently told me about his concerns that our Global North economies are not transitioning away from fossil fuels fast enough. "The IPCC report says we might already be past the 1.5 degrees Celsius that will lead to catastrophe!" he said. The 1.5-degree threshold for limiting warming on our planet was first laid out in the Paris Climate Accords in 2015 and is monitored by the Intergovernmental Panel on Climate Change, a global body of scientific experts. "The global average temperature is rising even faster than predicted."

"I know!" I snapped back, irrationally irate at this concerned person. "And whether it passes that point or doesn't, I'll be here living in that future, with my children." I like to think that I am a patient person, someone who can hold space for others to express fears and concerns. But in that moment, I had no space to hold anyone else's anxiety that the world will simply end if we cross those tipping points.

Because the world itself will not end. It is the filaments and tendrils of life on our planet—the human, plant, and animal worlds that it sustains—which are at risk from the changing climate. As my son assured me one day, we don't need to worry too much about being sucked into a giant black hole, because our sun has a relatively small mass and is unlikely to form a particularly large black hole. Our planet of rock and water will be just fine, spinning on its axis circling our sun for millions of foreseeable years. Unless, of course, the theory of the universe ending in a vacuum decay turns out to be true, and a quickly spreading bubble of vacuum decay happens to blink everything out of existence. Or a nefarious meteorite crashes into the planet, in which case it really may be the end of the world.

On one hand, we're suffering from too much water, as the polar ice caps melt into the ocean and the salty waters creep up over islands and coastlines around the world, pulling cities and whole cultures into the sea. Yet we're also suffering globally from not enough fresh water. Sometimes called the "third pole" of the world, the snow cover and glaciers of the strip of mountains in the Hindu Kush Himalayan region are the source of freshwater for a quarter of the world's population.[1] The Ganges, the Yangtze, the Mekong, and many other rivers throughout South Asia and China are connected to the water supply of the Himalayan region. This mountain region spans Afghanistan on the western side and continues east through Pakistan, India, China, Nepal, Bhutan, Bangladesh, and Myanmar. The water in these mountains, in the form of glaciers, snow, and permafrost, sustains life for people, plants, and animals across the Asian continent. But it is at grave risk of drying up as snowfall patterns change and glaciers melt at unprecedented rates.[2]

During the five years I lived in Nepal, I depended on this water for my daily needs. I crossed river canyons on swinging metal suspension bridges and met with farmers whose livelihoods depended on the water linked to the mountains and the cycles of monsoon that replenish the snows and irrigate the terraced fields. In my vacation time, I trekked up into the high Himalayas. I love the Annapurna region best for its stunning beauty and its diversity of human, animal, and plant life. Annapurna means "full of grain" in Nepali. This mountain range forms one part of the Himalayas, with lush green foothills winding up to the white peaks at the top of the world. Glacier-fed rivers and springs, along with the seasonal monsoon rains, feed fields of rice, buckwheat, and corn. I remember one October visit in particular, during the Dashain festival season when the fields were golden with ripened rice. Tall bamboo swings lashed together with ropes dotted the landscape, set up for playing and reveling in joy at the harvest season.

When I think of those villages below the glaciers, I am left wondering whether this heating climate will unleash, as seems inevitable, an overwhelming flood that will sweep away everything instantly in a glacial lake outburst as meltwater overflows the natural dams in the high mountain areas. Or if the foothills are somehow spared the flood, will the springs and rivers dry up as predicted, with significantly less water by 2100?

An old friend and colleague from my time in Nepal, Durga Sunchiuri, filled me in on how the climate crisis is intensifying in Nepal even in the span of the six years since I've moved back to Canada. Durga stayed at our home on one stop of his cross-Canada climate action advocacy speaking tour with Mennonite Central Committee, a nonprofit organization engaged in relief, development, and peacebuilding around the world. Shortly after he arrived, I went with Durga to a climate emergency vigil in the Waterloo public square. A group of about twenty figures bundled up in coats and hats cupped tealight candles in glass holders as they gathered in front of a single standing microphone and portable speaker.

The vigil, organized by a local interfaith climate advocacy group, was part of a series of vigils in the lead-up to COP28, the 2023 round of the United Nations Climate Change Conference where countries including Canada and Nepal negotiated emissions targets and contributions to the UN's Loss and Damage Fund. Historically high-emitting countries, including Canada, are now responsible to contribute financially to the countries, including Nepal, who are most affected by climate change yet have contributed the least to its cause.

My friend Durga shared stories of mountain villages whose springs have dried up, requiring mostly women and girls to spend hours carrying water from lower elevation rivers and springs. Insects affected by the changing conditions move to new territory, wreaking havoc on crops that never used to face pest challenges and bringing outbreaks of disease to new areas. Mosquito-borne dengue fever is sweeping higher-elevation areas of Nepal that previously were too cold for the mosquito species that transmits the virus. Rainfall comes unpredictably in cycles of drought and flooding. The Himalayas are visibly less snow-capped and more bare, with more rock face showing through.

It was jarring to compare the present and emerging water crisis in Nepal to the situation in Canada. Before the vigil that evening, we had sat around our dinner table with Durga chatting about my spouse's work in municipal carbon reduction. Luke is trying to convince hockey arenas to use a new technology to make the ice with cold water instead of hot water. Building the necessary buy-in is hard work. In Canada, where hockey is sacrosanct, arena managers are hesitant to try anything that might affect the ice quality. It feels absurd: that this is the level of discourse about climate change in our Canadian city, and that the energy and water resources needed to sustain this cultural fixture have any kind of priority in the global climate fight. Yet as winters in Canada become warmer, with more spikes and shifts in temperature, natural ice on ponds and outdoor hand-flooded rinks becomes more and more unreliable. In 2023, for the first time since it opened fifty years ago, the Rideau Canal in Ottawa, which becomes the world's longest skating rink in winter, didn't open for skating. The ice was too unstable. It's a mind-boggling cycle: energy overconsumption in Canada and other wealthy nations that is driving global climate change is increasing Canada's demand for energy to maintain its historically cold-climate traditions of skating and hockey.

Durga's short address at the vigil was followed by ten minutes of silent reflection. Shrugging my shoulders to brace myself against the late November chill, I thought about this vicious cycle of energy consumption and global impact as I watched my flickering candle struggle against the wind. Standing there in the town square, in a spot where the annual outdoor rink would be set up a few weeks later, hope for change felt as distant and hazy as the Himalayan peaks I used to glimpse from my home in the city of Kathmandu.

Green Party leader and member of Parliament Elizabeth May was a surprise speaker at the vigil that night. She reminded us that in the past, the world has acted together to protect the environment. Since controls were put in place through UN negotiations in the late 1980s, consumption of ozone-depleting substances has significantly decreased, and the hole in the ozone layer has peaked in size and is trending downward. Change is possible. Global cooperation on a large scale has happened and could happen again. The climate fight is not a lost cause. Still, in the volatility and shifting alliances of today's world order, global cooperation can sure seem unlikely.

It feels overwhelming—the magnitude of it all, and how small and powerless I feel to act. On my worst days I chuck empty peanut butter jars into the trash instead of doing the sticky work of washing them out for recycling. Because in light of the challenges brought about by our changing climate, what matter are two extra plastic containers in the landfill? They'll end up there eventually anyway. It's my bold act of defiance; why am I working so hard to reduce my personal use of plas-tics, to buy clothes secondhand, to eat less meat and dairy, to use the car less? My personal actions for a more sustainable, lower-carbon lifestyle feel like meaningless toil in the face of the global oil and gas industry and the violence of warfare that destroys people and the environment. As parents with two young kids who need lots of hands-on care amid the full weight of our work expectations, my spouse and I face long days and exhausted evenings just trying to keep everyone fed reasonably healthy food and do our best to keep on top of laundry, dishes, and the occasional vacuuming. At 9:36 on a Thursday evening, I don't have the energy or the willpower to wash out those jars anymore. It feels futile.

And still, the signals of our changing planet haunt me. A balmy 20-degree Celsius day in November feels sinister in its unseasonable warmth for Ontario. Sleet in May that unleashes a snow of falling cherry blossoms makes me wonder whether it is just bad luck or whether earlier, warmer springtime weather is drawing the blossoms out too soon, making them vulnerable. I plant milkweed, marigolds, zinnias, and other butterfly-friendly species, hoping to welcome the monarchs on their way; some years I've seen a few monarchs and a handful of other butterflies, but this past summer I saw a lone monarch in my garden. I was equal parts delighted to see this orange-and-black visitor and unsettled that it was late August and I had seen only this one. The challenges facing us in the present and the future push me to apathy, disengagement, and despair. Sometimes it is too much to hold.

I'm not alone in this unsettledness, a constant hum of grief and worry about what we humans are doing to each other and to life on our planet. Climate anxiety, as this feeling has come to be called, is a rational response to the multiplying effects of climate change. In a 2021 *Lancet Planetary Health* study of young people in ten countries, researchers found that two-thirds were very or extremely worried about climate change, and three-quarters said they think the future is frightening. The study authors stress that these are rational responses to the threats facing us globally, yet they also note that this burden of anxiety and worry takes a toll on mental health in a way that is not easily solved.[3]

Somehow, we have to find our way forward, through what feels overwhelming, to take action anyway. One of the insidious things about despair is that it is paralyzing. It assumes that the outcome is fixed, that nothing can change it. Especially when the challenges feel so huge and so distant from us, despair can lead to disengagement and apathy—these feelings that so many of us struggle with. Paradoxically, facing these challenges with eternal optimism can also lead to the same place of disengagement and apathy. If you think everything will turn out fine, why take any action at all? Perhaps the only way forward is with a gritty, grounded kind of hope, one that looks clear-eyed at the challenges and is willing to take the next step, and the next, to act in accordance with our values regardless of whether the outcome seems fixed.

It reminds me of the women—Mary Magdalene, Joanna, and others—who showed up at the grave after Jesus' crucifixion, doing the tending and ritual that needed to be done, showing their faithfulness in small actions despite their despair and heartbreak (Luke 24). They were not trying to avoid their anguish—their very acts were an expression of it. They were just trying to keep on anyway. They kept showing up even when it seemed like the story was over. Because that is hope: not that you are optimistic or positive about the future but that you show up anyway, taking the next necessary step to move toward the potential of a future of flourishing and well-being.

For many of us, we know how to live differently in a warming and conflicted world and are taking steps to do so in our daily lives. But in our quest for being good, for doing things right, we can get so caught up in trying to make changes in our own lives that our energy and focus shift from the centers of power where needed systemic change can occur. I wonder how Doris Longacre Janzen, author of the iconic 1976 *More-with-Less* cookbook, might feel about where we are today. Her book on cooking and eating simple meals, with lifestyle suggestions to live more lightly on the earth, is more relevant than ever. It's a guide for North Americans to shift away from a food consumption lifestyle that requires five Earths to sustain it. It has sold nearly one million copies, finding traction with people looking to live and eat differently than the culture of consumption around them. But decades on from its publication by the very same publisher of this book, we're still bringing cloth bags to the grocery store and finding three ways to use a leftover chicken carcass while the world is burning. On the one hand, this could look like a failure of the book's vision. But we can also look at these small, personal changes—transforming the habits of readers, one at a time—as something worthwhile regardless of larger outcomes.

We need both the ways of living as if the future we want is here and the understanding that we're in the imperfect space of the not-yet. We need to have grace for ourselves while we keep the focus on bigger advocacy goals that can have a longer-term impact beyond one household's consumption patterns, such as advocacy to expand city public transportation and cycling infrastructure, and pressure on federal governments to make progress on global emissions reduction targets. In small and big ways, we have to keep taking the next necessary step and not lose sight of what must change if the future is to be different from the trajectory it is on.

Sometimes our small actions are more about a personal commitment to a different way of living than about tangible impact—and this is especially important in the face of a crisis that none of us can solve individually. One of my most memorable experiences of living into these kinds of small changes was when my family traveled by riverboat from Bangladesh's capital city of Dhaka to the Bay of Bengal and the Sundarbans mangrove forest. *Sundarban* means "beautiful forest," and it is. Mangrove forests that grow in the mix of salty and fresh water play a critical role in mitigating flooding. The water flowing through the river to the mangrove forests and eventually the sea in the Bay of Bengal has its source in the Himalayas. From the riverboat, it was hard to imagine the water's journey from the icy mountains to the heat that feels like a force of gravity in the humid climate of the Sundarbans.

Luke and I were living in Nepal at the time, working for Mennonite Central Committee and learning what it meant to parent three-month-old Isaac. This included handwashing cloth diapers in one of the boat's tiny bathrooms and hanging them up to dry on a clothesline strung along the side of the boat. It's hard to keep up with a baby's "output" even with a washing machine. To do it on the boat took time and effort, and I questioned whether it was worth it. Yet when I thought of the alternative of tossing disposable diapers into the Sundarbans, there was no question. For those four days, as Luke and I took turns scrubbing cotton prefolds in a plastic bucket in a hot, muggy bathroom, it became a spiritual discipline, one of choosing to care for the earth through an intense practice. Did our actions have much of a tangible impact on the Sundarbans? No. But it heightened my awareness of and connectedness to the world around me. And it was an act of hope—a tangible step of living into a future in which my daily actions support life rather than pollute it.

While the scale of global climate change that we are experiencing may be unprecedented, the story of humanity is one of people facing adversity over and over again and still finding the strength to go on. Story and history preserve these memories, a wellspring of strength to draw on as we face unique challenges. When the grief for our hurting world falls heaviest on me, I find myself turning to writers and stories of people and cultures living in the hard times of grief, terror, and loss to learn from their wisdom as I seek my own way forward.

The Bible is full of such stories. The story about the courageous midwives Shiphrah and Puah, found in Exodus 1:15–21, is one of my favorites. These women undertook ordinary acts of extraordinary courage. Shiphrah and Puah were midwives who chose everyday actions of courage and resistance. They chose life in the face of death and destruction after Pharaoh, fearing the growing Hebrew population, ordered the midwives to kill any male babies they delivered. The text says that Shiphrah and Puah, fearing God, "did not do as the king of Egypt commanded them, but they let the boys live." When Pharaoh questioned them, Shiphrah and Puah said, "The Hebrew women are not like the Egyptian women, for they are vigorous and give birth before the midwife comes to them."

Shiphrah and Puah were not rulers or authorities, but they knew the power they had to save lives, and they used it despite the risks. To do so, they drew on all the negative stereotypes against Hebrew women for their benefit—and somehow, the Egyptian authorities believed them: *Guess these midwives are just not very competent. Maybe even a bit lazy about getting out to births. Guess Hebrew women really are somehow more fit for heavy manual labor and childbearing than Egyptian women.* Armed with their wits, Shiphrah and Puah did what they could so that as many children as possible would survive.

It's not clear from the original Hebrew text whether Shiphrah and Puah were Hebrew themselves. Were they Egyptian women who served as midwives to the Hebrew women, showing up as allies? We only know that they countered a genocide of the Hebrew people. Ethnicity was patrilineal, so in the context of the ancient Near East, wiping out the boys would eventually have meant wiping out the whole ethnic group.

This pattern, of women doing everyday things as acts of resistance and justice, continues in Exodus 2: Pharaoh, stymied by the midwives, then ordered all baby boys thrown into the Nile. Moses's mother bravely hid her baby in the river, and her daughter Miriam watched over him. Pharaoh's daughter discovered the baby, and though she knew that the baby was one of the Hebrews, she chose to adopt him. These ordinary acts, of attending births and caring for children in vulnerable situations, are ultimately what God used to deliver God's people through Moses. It could not have happened without this network of care and solidarity. These women did what they could to save lives in the face of a massacre.

Other ordinary acts of extraordinary courage in the Bible include Mary's act of hope to bear and raise a child, something that is always miraculous and mundane, and never without risk. Her Magnificat, found in Luke 1:46–55, is one of the most beautiful expressions of claiming hope amid hardship and despair. It is a song of living under occupation and experiencing gender oppression that threatened Mary's life as she risked a pregnancy while unwed.

Theologian Nancy Elizabeth Bedford points to the calling of the fishermen—Jesus' first disciples—and how their choices to follow Jesus were concrete, material acts of hope in the face of the pressures of the Roman Empire and what that meant for their precarious livelihood. For the fishermen who encountered Jesus and took steps to live differently, discipleship—becoming and being a follower of Jesus—was less about believing certain things and more about "following [Jesus] in specific contexts, in concrete, material ways that are traversed with hope."[4]

Shiphrah, Puah, Miriam, and Pharaoh's daughter would not have used the term *discipleship*, but their concrete actions toward material well-being, toward claiming hope in the face of despair, are embodied examples of it. Their choices led to liberatory outcomes even though the outcomes were hardly conceivable at the time of action. Mary and the women who showed up at the tomb out of their fear and grief took the steps forward that were in their power to do. And those steps led to good things, unimaginably good things, even though they were still enmeshed within systems of violence, domination, and oppression. Their hardship and the suffering didn't miraculously disappear, but along the journey of faithfully showing up, new, life-giving possibilities emerged.

Suffering is part of the origin of my family history and the history of the faith tradition that I follow, even as it has been complicit in the suffering of others. So how did my faith ancestors, the early Anabaptists who faced persecution and martyrdom for daring to challenge the status quo in sixteenth-century Europe, maintain hope amid a bleak and uncertain future? In search of this answer, I pulled out a book that I've held on to since a long-ago university class on early Anabaptism. It has one of the longest book titles I've ever encountered: *The Earliest Hymns of the Ausbund: Some Beautiful Christian Songs Composed and Sung in the Prison at Passau, Published in 1546.*

The hymns in this collection were written between 1535 and about 1537 by a group of Anabaptist refugees captured on their journey from Moravia to South Germany and then held in the dungeons at Passau, Germany. Under pressure of mental and physical torture, and fully expecting to be executed like many Anabaptists before them, this group of weavers, tailors, and artisans-turned-spiritual leaders wrote and sang their faith witness and testimony. Fifty-three of these songs, all set to folk melodies and common tunes, made it out of the prison and were later published as the *Ausbund*. They still form part of the hymnal used by Old Order Amish groups today. For the prisoners, singing was a practice of mutual solidarity and a form of group encouragement, cementing their bonds and strengthening each other to resist the pressure to recant and distance themselves from Anabaptism as the state authorities wanted. Another account of early Anabaptists singing includes a record from 1529, in Alzey on the Rhine, north of Strasbourg, noting that 350 Anabaptist prisoners "responded with such joyful singing that their enemies outside became much more fearful than the prisoners inside."[5]

Paging through *The Earliest Hymns of the Ausbund*, I see themes of joy amid suffering and the hope of union with the divine, calls to stay faithful and to endure with love in the face of fear and hardship. From hymn 87, stanza 15:

> Wherever love has been poured, it drives away fear.
> Since fear has pain and also distress,
> it cannot abide with love.
> Since God's love has no pain,
> wherever it is,
> there is great joy for all time.
> It turns suffering into joy.[6]

During five years of imprisonment in Passau, some died of disease and mistreatment. Others later recanted their faith or were let out on bail when a more lenient ruler came along. There was no happy ending. Yet their words live on and have fueled this movement through the centuries. The hymns, with their radical critique of the religious establishment and stark callout of the hypocrisy of religious officials in holding on to power and wealth while claiming to follow Jesus, were so threatening that even in 1692, more than 150 years after their writing, the *Ausbund* remained on the list of banned books in Berne, Switzerland, that should be confiscated by the authorities if found.[7] Sometimes the stories we are living form parts of larger struggles, larger stories, that we can't fathom amid our daily struggles in the present.

Records from Augsburg in 1527 and 1528 show how women in particular supported the growth of the persecuted movement through housing and feeding Anabaptist refugees, contributing money and goods to the common purse, and hosting sewing circles that clandestinely brought women together for conversation and learning. In their grocery stalls and cobbler's shops, they organized, tended, and supported the movement, using what they had to build a network of communication and care.[8] Lived discipleship—the idea that faith is something embedded in our daily actions, that faith is something that is done as much as believed—was core to the spirituality of the early Anabaptists, and it continues to be so in the tradition today. I'm coming to understand that it is in the living out, the doing, that I find hope in the face of despair. Hope emerges on the journey of taking action, of living out core beliefs and values in everyday choices—especially in challenging times.

Hope matters because it keeps us going. It keeps us surviving and dreaming that things can be different from how they are. Hope is the faith and belief that another way of living, another way of existing together on this planet, is possible. In the face of the climate crisis, giving up in despair is the worst possible outcome. Despair means giving up, accepting that how things are is how they have to be. Tending the embers of hope, fueling the sparks and flames that grow and falter and grow again, is our essential task. As I engage more deeply in this struggle, the further I move into joy and meaning and beauty amid suffering, into grounded hope that keeps going in the face of despair. Dreaming, imagining, creating, tending . . . these are all ways of living the world we want into being. If we can't do this in little ways, home ways, community and family ways, how would we do it in big ways? We have to practice and build it, over and over again. Hope is the courage to show up for the ordinary actions, believing that something else is possible. Taking the next step, and the next, toward what could be.

My worst days aren't easy. But on some of my best days, it is taking simple, hopeful actions that keep me feeling rooted and grounded. It's finding joy in riding my bike on the trails and newly developed bike lanes to get around the city. It's taking the commuter train into Toronto because it's so much more pleasant than driving the crowded highways. It's showing up with others for acts of care and solidarity, like bringing food to friends who've had babies or lost family members. It's living in a way that centers community, people, and connection to the land not because "we have to fight climate change" but because living this way brings life.

I almost didn't go to the climate emergency vigil with my friend Durga. I was tired. I had worked late and missed putting my kids to bed other nights that week. It was a blustery evening in late fall. But I wanted to keep Durga company and hear what he had to say. And I was curious about the climate vigils. Other friends had found them meaningful and, knowing my interest in climate justice, had suggested that I check it out.

That evening, the vigil organizers might have been discouraged. There were only ten or so people there when things got going, about twenty all told by the end. But the space they created that night brought together Durga, sharing about the impact of climate change on Nepal on a cross-Canada speaking tour with Mennonite Central Committee, with Green Party MP Elizabeth May, a Canadian politician attending the UN's climate summit. It's an unlikely story of crossing paths. And it's a story about faithfully showing up for change in small, concrete ways, of doing what is possible and knowing that the outcomes could be unexpectedly transformative.

The coronavirus pandemic expanded our collective vocabulary of grief to understand that we can grieve for the loss of a dream, a plan, a future, just as much as we can grieve for real people, places, and things that have passed away and are lost to us. I'm coming to think of grief as an experience of love— for what was, what could have been, and what could be. It can take the form of anger; lately, when I find myself feeling angry, I look deeper and find that underneath that flare of heat is a river of grief. My anger at others for what I perceive to be a lack of concern about the state of the world and our relationships with each other in it is often a cover for my sadness that things are not different. Sometimes that grief takes the form of anger at myself for not living up to my expectations.

What am I grieving? What am I angry about, and whom or what am I angry with? Examining my emotions gives me information about what I care about, what visions I hold of a good future for myself, for other humans, and for our larger network of kin in creation. In the book *Active Hope*, ecophilosopher Joanna Macy and resilience specialist Chris Johnstone offer a key to unlocking these questions within ourselves: "As with grief work, facing our distress doesn't make it disappear. Instead, when we do face it, we are able to place our distress within a larger landscape that gives it a different meaning. Rather than feeling afraid of our pain for the world we learn to be strengthened by it."[9] What a beautiful idea. Instead of running away from the pain and hardship of the world, the grief we feel, and the despair at change that seems impossible, we can grow our heart muscles to expand and hold the pain. We can allow it to take us deeper into our longing and dreaming for what could be but is not yet.

Instead of putting up more walls to protect myself, letting in only a little at a time, I am working on softening and expanding my inner resources to look clear-eyed at the pain and loss I feel to guide my actions forward, along with others. To hold space for love to make its home within me, to turn suffering into joy not by ignoring it but by holding it in the light of love, as my Anabaptist forebears did in the face of fear and death.

This journey of discipleship—seeking to follow Jesus' call to live in love, to seek peace and justice for the marginalized, and to imagine a world of transformed relationships—calls me to go deeper into our present reality. In the book *Who Was Jesus and What Does It Mean to Follow Him?*, theologian Nancy Elizabeth Bedford writes, "The way of Jesus is marked by many joys, but also by the difficulties and obstacles intrinsic to pushing back against the false gods of capitalism, militarism, racism, classism, sexism, and all the other forces that require the sacrifice of human lives to continue to consolidate their hold on humans."[10] As she notes, there is a cost to discipleship.

There is suffering and there is joy, just as the prison songs of the Anabaptists held in Passau's dungeon testify.

In their handbook for organizing and movement-building, Kelly Hayes and Mariame Kaba draw on decades of activist work in the prison abolition movement. They advise those who want to enter into the hard and necessary work of the struggle for social change and justice to create space to practice hope and to practice grief. These concepts are not opposites; both call us to reject apathy and indifference to the state of the world. And both call us into community to experience them together in a transformative way. As Hayes and Kaba write, "We do not need to believe that everything will work out in the end. We need only decide who we are choosing to be and how we are choosing to function in relation to the outcome we desire and abide by what those decisions demand of us."[11]

That is a freeing thought. We don't have to see all the way to the ending—just toward the next steps—to make a flourishing future, a livable future for people and all creation, a reality. We don't have to do everything alone. We need only take the steps ahead of us according to the values we care about, trusting that even though not everything will work out, the steps we take—the seeds we plant—can make that livable future just a little more possible. Seeds planted in the soil of history, in grief and hope, in mutuality and interdependence as we turn toward others for care and support just as we offer ourselves in return. Seeds planted in the spirit of humility and wonder: we are an interconnected part of an unknowably vast universe with the power to influence it in our daily living.

The actions of one person alone did not get us into this mess. It will require more than individual actions to get out of it. It is increasingly clear to me that this work can only be done in community with others. It doesn't really matter whether I feel optimistic or pessimistic, or whether I define my internal mental state as hopeful or despairing. What matters is the commitment to keep showing up with others, to believing together that it is worth striving for things to be different from how they are. To begin living together as if the future we want is here. We need the moral support of community, the feeling of belonging to something bigger, the relationships in which we find joy and companionship along the journey, people to mourn with and people to rejoice with. To make the kind of changes at the scale we need, this work needs bigger and broader coalitions of people who learn from and challenge each other to go deeper into care and possibility, weaving together the fabric of community we need to live the alternative futures we imagine into being. I am not alone; we are not alone. We do this together, embedded in the miraculous hospitality of our planetary home that sustains the only life we know to exist anywhere in the universe. Holding on to connection, relationship, and joy even in, especially in, times of suffering and grief.

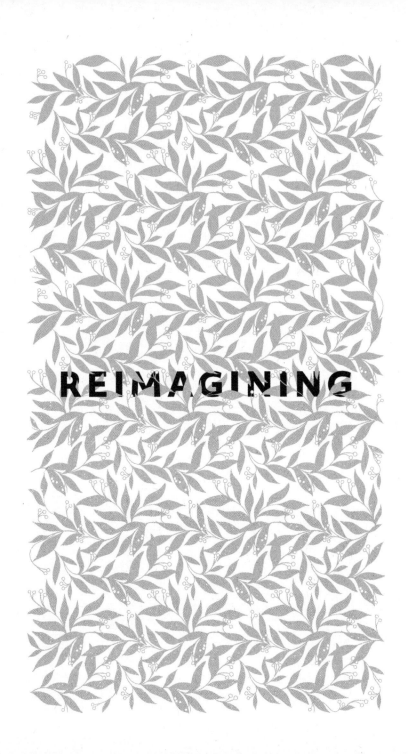

REIMAGINING

5

REIMAGINING LEADERSHIP

Gaining a new perspective can feel like an earthquake that shatters your existing views. And sometimes it takes a literal earthquake to change the way you see the world. That's how it was for me—feeling the ground swell and roll beneath my feet gave me a glimpse of the kind of interconnected leadership that will be necessary if we hope to move forward together toward courageous change for people and planet.

It was the kind of bright May day when the wind blows the smog out of the Kathmandu Valley. Purple jacaranda trees bloomed in the dusty streets against a clean sky with hints of Himalayan peaks shrouded in clouds at the northern horizon. My colleagues and I had just finished a lunch of *momo* dumplings and fried rice. We were walking back to the Nepal head office of the North American-based charity we worked for when the ground started rolling and swelling beneath our feet. The weird groan and rumble of the earthquake filled my ears as I scanned for falling electricity poles, crumbling walls, and off-balance rooftop water tanks while we stumbled along the brick-walled lane to an open lot across from the office's gated yard.

"This should not be happening, this should *not* be happening!" a colleague exclaimed.

But it was happening. Despite all the public messaging that the aftershocks would decline in strength and another major earthquake was highly unlikely, a 7.3-magnitude earthquake jolted us again on May 12, 2015. This was just weeks after a 7.8-magnitude earthquake had shifted the block of the earth's crust that carries Kathmandu south by ten feet in thirty seconds. Between the two earthquakes and more than five hundred aftershocks, over nine thousand people died, and many more were injured. Ancient temple sites and the distinctive architecture of medieval cityscapes, including parts of Kathmandu, pancaked into grey piles of debris. Many rural areas were hard hit as well. In some parts, entire villages collapsed and were left with no road access for relief materials. It was a human, cultural, and environmental tragedy. And as always, the greatest impact was on economically marginalized communities, who bore the brunt of vulnerability.

After the first earthquake, the way forward had felt clear. At least, as clear as possible when you find yourself living through a major disaster. You act; you take the next necessary step, and the next one, and the next one after that until a new kind of normal takes hold and you work toward what you hope is possible for yourself and the people around you. By this time in May, our team had moved forward from the early days of the crisis, going beyond meeting personal daily survival needs to a new normal of planning relief and reconstruction activities with Nepali partner organizations. We were tentatively moving back into our office building, which appeared to have no structural damage, and we were getting on with the huge task of launching a major disaster response. This second quake revived all the fear and trauma of the first quake and left me wondering whether everything we had worked so hard for in the past weeks had just been undone by escalating tragedy.

When the ground grew calm again, I was at a loss. I stood still in the green space of the open lot looking around at my Nepali, Canadian, and American team members, thinking, *I have no idea what happens now.* It was a defining moment of leadership as I felt the weight of my role as codirector of our organization's program in Nepal. I could sense everyone looking at me. I had to *do something.* But as I remained frozen in place, others moved into action around me. As it turns out, I did not, in fact, have to singlehandedly decide what to do next.

Luke and I had moved to Nepal in the summer of '69—2069 in Nepal's official Bikram Sambat calendar, that is, which corresponds to 2012 in the Roman calendar system. That year the Bryan Adams song "Summer of '69" was on repeat, playing everywhere in the Thamel backpacker district and a favorite of tourist bar cover bands. When the earthquakes struck, we had been living in Nepal for three years. I had studied the Nepali language to a full working proficiency, I had traveled extensively with NGOs and rural development organizations across the country, and I had been promoted from food security advisor to co–country director, taking on the mantle of in-country leadership for the organization's relief, development, and peace work.

Leadership in community was a defining hallmark of my experience in Nepal, and it was highlighted most in the earthquake response. It took the form of action through embedded networks and relationships. Although our presence was small compared to large international charities like World Vision and Care International, the strength of our networked connections and relationships allowed us to move quickly and efficiently to reach highly affected people who needed material aid and were far from the more accessible urban areas. We had long-established relationships with local partners chosen for an alignment between our values and process, and this network was ready to move information and resources to connect international aid with affected communities. As a team of partnering organizations, we took pride in being the first external relief response to reach a remote district. There was a strong foundation for a shared, distributed leadership model, a model with no room for heroes.

It's not a coincidence, I think, that a shared leadership model looks something like the tree networks that support the strength of a forest. Ecologist and professor Suzanne Simard has changed how we think about trees and their role in sustaining ecosystems. She discovered that trees communicate with each other to warn of pests and to share nutrients. Some trees, known as "hub trees" or "mother trees," play a larger role in resourcing younger saplings. Similar in structure to the neural networks in our brains, mycorrhizal fungi form an underground web between roots, sometimes called the "wood wide web," allowing water and nutrients to pass between trees. In this way older trees pass on energy and information that help new seedlings grow and thrive.[1]

I like to imagine the partnership web we relied on after the earthquake like the network of roots and fungi that sustains the rhododendron forest on the high-altitude slopes of the Himalayas—a resilient network for sharing information and resources. Trusted relationships, a desire to help each other, and cell phones allowed this network to thrive. After the earthquake, for example, partner organizations in less affected parts of the country near the Indian border visited local markets, factories, and warehouses to scope out relief materials. They shared about possible resources with NGO staff in Kathmandu who were planning relief responses in the mountains. Leaders and community organizations identified and prioritized emergency relief needs in rural areas; partners and team members in Kathmandu made project plans and proposals for funding and coordinated with other organizations to minimize duplication. My role was to connect the Nepal country office and our Canadian headquarters. I also spent many early mornings and late nights doing newspaper, radio, and television interviews with Canadian and American news outlets to promote international fundraising efforts. It was networked collaboration on a massive scale, and it worked.

This was not a conflict-free process. One such conflict between the teams in Nepal and Canada was over the use of roofing nails. The team in Canada was mandated to ensure that our humanitarian work in Nepal met all the best-practice standards for aid. They had to sign off on all our proposals for quality assurance. The local partner we were working with to reach a remote, highly affected, and under-resourced area learned that temporary shelter materials were urgently needed. The monsoon rainy season would arrive any day. Many of the stone and earth mortar buildings in the community had been badly damaged, and residents lacked shelter. In the coming months, heavy rains and landslides on the mountainous unpaved roads were sure to cut off road access until the roads could be cleared and repaired again after the monsoon.

Our partner organization proposed a relief project to fund zinc sheets for roofing, tarps, and sleeping mats. The community's practice, widespread in Nepal, was to use strips of bamboo and rope to fasten the zinc sheeting for a roof. This simple solution meant that the zinc sheets were infinitely reusable and could be repurposed from temporary shelter into permanent roofing material once houses could be safely reconstructed. Yet this practice was at odds with the global standard for emergency shelter materials and construction that my Canada-based colleagues required in order to sign off on the aid funding. The "best practice" guidelines required the provision of roofing nails and direction to securely nail down the zinc sheets. Community members pointed out that once nails were put into the zinc roofing sheets, they could not be reused without leaks.

It was a tense week of emails and phone calls, spanning the eleven-hour-and-forty-five-minute time difference between Kathmandu and Winnipeg and involving many conversations between the partner organizations and local government officials in Kathmandu and various communities. I checked the weather forecast repeatedly, tracking the arrival of the monsoon rains across South Asia and hoping that the window for delivering the relief supplies would stay open long enough. We eventually convinced our colleagues in Canada of the utility and safety of this practice, and the network of partnerships purchased the materials and got them into the community before the rains started. After a day of travel over rough roads and across riverbeds, the trucks of blankets, mats, and zinc roofing sheets finally arrived after dark in the mountainous community. The supplies were unloaded by the light of the truck headlights that silhouetted tall corn plants growing in the fields by the road.

The weeks and months after the earthquakes were a difficult time, one of the most stressful periods of my life, and certainly one of the most challenging times for practicing leadership. I was three months pregnant with Isaac and in the throes of morning sickness when the quakes struck. I lived on potato chips, watermelon, and plums that spring and summer. Yet what stands out to me most from that time nearly a decade ago are the relationships and the resilience of that partner web. As a leader, my work was more about spinning spiderwebs of connection than about accomplishing objectives. We faced difficult decisions about how and where to allocate resources and what partnerships to pursue. As a staff, we carefully set criteria with lots of consultation at all levels, prioritizing the needs and assets of those most directly affected. What other aid groups were already active in a community? Who was falling through the gaps in relief efforts? What did highly affected people say was their biggest challenge? What partner organizations had the infrastructure and relationship networks to manage larger projects and move forward quickly? I didn't always get it right, and neither did others on the team. The magic was in our interconnected web. It was not up to any individual alone but was something owned by all of us.

This kind of leadership is critical as we find our way forward in the Anthropocene. How will we make the kind of changes necessary to adapt in ways that lead to flourishing for all, and how will we make decisions without reproducing the inequalities that have led us into this mess in the first place? How can leadership practices lead us to interconnected thriving that is good for people and our natural environment?

When we think about "leadership" in the natural world, we often think of competition: survival of the fittest, of trees competing for light and resources in a forest. But that is not always the case. As we see in the example of mycorrhizal networks, scientists are learning that nature is much more complexly intertwined than previously known. Western scientific ways of knowing are slowly arriving at what Indigenous cultures have long understood: everything is interconnected and interdependent. In a forest, the biodiversity of tree and plant species strengthens resilience and is a resource for self-healing. Having many species, each with unique profiles of strength and vulnerabilities, enables a forest to adapt to changing and challenging conditions like forest fires, droughts, and pests. By identifying and supporting hub trees, for example, we can help forests self-heal from human impacts and aid forests' adaptation to climate change.

Hub trees provide a helpful metaphor for a model of interconnected leadership that leads to resilient and thriving systems. Hub trees are resource repositories for their networks, increasing survival and resiliency to threats for the whole forest. In a forest, diversity and interconnection is resilience. Applying this model to human systems, a leader is someone who takes responsibility for sharing information and resources to benefit the whole. A leader is part of a network of leaders, some visible and some invisible, all working to nourish, repair, heal, and share across the fabric of the community. As we learn from forest ecology, cultivating diversity builds resilience and adaptability in systems. Rather than ask how we are establishing our own strength, we might instead ask how we are sharing resources and building the complexity and strength of interconnections.

This is a stark contrast to the individualistic myth of the hero-leader that is so pervasive in Western society. Heroes and champions are at the center of our stories, capturing our imaginations. That bright spring day in Kathmandu as I stood paralyzed in the aftermath of the second major earthquake, why did I feel pressure to respond immediately? Why did I think being a leader meant leaping into action? In the champion versus champion model, leadership becomes a public contest of power. We pursue competing visions of change to exert control and influence over a community or society.

No wonder, then, that polarization is on the rise across our society. In fact, encouraging polarization—which often takes the form of casting a collective "other" as a morally deficient villain—is a highly effective tool in this contest of power. A hero-leader is best served when people create and shape their identities in narrower and narrower ways until every differing view is experienced as a personal attack on oneself. Leadership becomes primarily about defining and broadcasting an identity that others either adopt as part of their own or reject as fundamentally opposed to it. Any challenge to the hero-leader's ideas automatically casts the challenger as a villain.

Moisés Naím, a scholar, journalist, and the former executive director of the World Bank, links growing polarization to the rise of celebrity culture and the era of politics as entertainment. "As politics devolves into pure spectacle, people begin to relate to their political leaders the same way they relate to their favorite entertainers and sports stars," he writes in *The Revenge of Power*. "The key question becomes not 'What are they doing?' but rather 'Who's winning?'"[2]

This polarizing model of entertainment-focused leadership driven by individual charisma and narrowly defined identity spills out of the political realm into all facets of how we come together in civil society organizations, faith communities, movements, and societies. It shapes expectations of what it means to be a leader, and expectations of what interactions with leaders look like.

In Christian churches and faith-based organizations and movements, the hero-champion mentality can take the shape of people claiming the role of prophet—a divinely inspired countercultural champion proclaiming the way of the Lord. It adds a layer of spirituality that is meant to imply God's favor. For who can challenge a prophet? Add in the impact of patriarchy and white supremacy culture, and it's a recipe for unchecked saviorism in climate activism, social justice movements, and churches. This model allows no room for accountability, for learning and growth. There is only the charismatic prophet and their followers, driven to forward their vision at any cost. Any challenge to the leader's actions can be framed as disloyalty to the movement, thereby shutting down legitimate concerns and preventing accountability.

The individual focus of this model particularly disadvantages those with less power in a society or community. Individuals are held to unequal standards. In North America, study after study shows that women and minorities are held to different standards than White men. A 2022 study on women in the workforce found that women and minorities continue to be drastically underrepresented in corporate leadership: 61 percent of C-suite roles were held by White men, 21 percent by White women, 13 percent by men of color, and 5 percent by women of color. The data do not report on other genders, LGBTQ2S+ identity, or disability as categories, but intersecting identities further amplify inequities and oppression. According to the research, women "are far more likely than men leaders to have colleagues question their judgment or imply that they aren't qualified for their jobs." These undermining behaviors are most pronounced in the experience of Black women leaders, who reported much higher rates of people questioning their qualifications, of being mistaken for a more junior employee, and of having their judgment questioned than male leaders or female leaders in general.[3]

While this kind of questioning is often attributed to age—itself another form of discrimination—a study published in the *Harvard Business Review* found that women face this kind of discrimination at every age. Although many women experience ageism in the workplace, the study found that there is no "right age" for women in leadership and professional roles to not face age-related discrimination. Women may be discounted for being too young and inexperienced, or for being past their prime and seen as lacking in fresh ideas. Their leadership was always open to age-based questioning no matter what their age. "There was always an age-based excuse to not take women seriously, to discount their opinions, or to not hire or promote them," the study authors write.[4]

These problems affect both leaders and the organizations they serve. In a report on the future of nonprofit and public service leadership, leaders and organizations named that current leadership models and organizational structures are facing a variety of challenges: declining trust in institutions, growing polarization, increased awareness of burnout and need to prioritize wellness in order to sustain staff. Echoing the findings of the studies named in the previous paragraphs, the report noted that "BIPOC [Black, Indigenous, and people of color] leaders felt like their leadership legitimacy was being questioned because they were not a 'straight white male.'

Younger senior leaders spoke of not being taken seriously due to their age and mentioned looking forward to aging so their leadership [would not be] called into question as often."[5]

I have experienced this in my own leadership work. In one role, where my gender and age differed from most of my colleagues, I found myself resorting to behind-the-scenes strategies to influence decision-making. When asked to comment on a change in program structure, I first called an older, White, male colleague to discuss my concerns. I asked him to bring my ideas to the group so that I could publicly second his response and better ensure that my proposed changes would then be accepted by others. I was afraid that if I raised my concerns directly, I would get pushback from some in the group and be told that once again I wasn't listening enough to others' opinions. I should stop pushing my agenda. When I realized how much I was working behind the scenes to influence the outcomes through others because I was concerned about being penalized for bringing them forward directly, I decided I needed to step away from that space. No one should have to walk on eggshells to preserve other people's egos or feel that they need to feed their ideas to colleagues with more social power in order for those ideas to be accepted and acted on. A healthy team or organization must create space for many ideas and many approaches to leadership to flourish. Failing to do so risks losing out on crucial voices and perspectives.

Kim Campbell, who served as Canadian prime minister for six months in 1993, the first and thus far only woman to hold the role, named the difficulty of showing up as a leader with an underrepresented identity. "When you are not prototypical—when you are not like the others who have done the job—it becomes very difficult for people to overcome their visceral sense that something is not quite right," she said. "The only way to change this is to change the landscape from which people get their sense of how the world works."[6]

Can we imagine a world where no one is limited by gender, sexual orientation, race, age, or ability, or left wondering whether they are experiencing different treatment because of some facet of their identity? It will require transformative, systemic changes—both to our leadership structures and to our expectations of leaders—to have hope for a truly flourishing future.

In some ways, the concept of interconnected leadership as opposed to individual-focused leadership feels self-protective—as if there is no space for people with marginalized identities to stand out and shine, as if they must instead take strength in numbers and hide their true glow. Does this concept of interconnected, networked leadership focus too much on protective strategies when what we really want is freedom?

We can look again to the wisdom of the forest. A forest can have many beautiful, tall, thriving trees. Biodiversity is a strength. The more some trees succeed, the more others do as well. We, too, can reimagine the nature of leadership so that there is space for many to flourish. The goal of healthy leadership should be the thriving and well-being of the whole. As we move into this time of climate crisis and rising global economic inequalities and instability, the world doesn't need more heroes. Heroes alone cannot solve our problems, big as they are. The world needs more allies, partners, backers, and collaborators willing to work together to make change happen.

In the introduction to their edited collection of essays on the climate crisis, marine biologist Ayana Elizabeth Johnson and activist Katharine K. Wilkinson make the bold and necessary claim that the climate crisis *is* a leadership crisis. It's not that we lack knowledge of what to do to stop the climate crisis; the problem is that the necessary changes and actions are not happening. *Who* makes decisions and *how* we make decisions must change if we are to succeed in the kinds of social transformations that are needed in the coming critical decade. We need a true diversity of voices at the table with all of our valuable perspectives, ideas, and solutions, particularly those who are most affected by existing vulnerabilities and social inequities. Addressing equity and inclusion in how we respond to the challenges ahead must be the first priority. As Johnson and Wilkinson write, "Equity is not secondary to survival, as some suggest; it is survival."[7]

Leadership must be about making change, not about being in charge. This cannot happen effectively in a linear, objectives-focused approach. To drive genuine change, leadership must "strategically build linkages and coordinate with and across not-like-minded and not-like-situated relational spaces," writes peace scholar and practitioner John Paul Lederach. He describes this as the "web approach," which thinks not "in terms of us-vs.-them, but rather about the nature of the change sought and how multiple sets of interdependent processes will link people and place to move the whole of the system toward those changes." For Lederach, the central question is, "Who has to find a way to be connected to whom?"[8] This is why an interconnected, decentralized approach to leadership matters. For the change and social transformation that we need to address the climate crisis, it depends on building connections, links, webs, that can surface visions for change and mobilize resources where they are needed for that change to happen. It is power held in community.

What does it look like to put these ideas into practice? Many movements, coalitions, and grassroots organizations working for social and environmental change have been developing leadership cultures that reflect their visions of a more just, interconnected society. One such organization is UPROSE, the oldest Latino-based community organization in Brooklyn, New York, which describes itself as "an intergenerational, multi-racial, nationally-recognized, women of color-led, grassroots organization that promotes sustainability and resiliency through community organizing, education, leadership development, and cultural/artistic expression." Elizabeth Yeampierre, executive director, offers an alternative vision of interconnected leadership:

> We have to be, right now, in deep solidarity with each other and we have to be able to build cultural practice that is built on collaboration. We [at UPROSE are] leaderful and matriarchal. . . . Matriarchal because the way that matriarchy makes decisions is more collective and more inclusive and allows for space. If you're sick, if you have to take care of your children, whatever is happening, you are [still] part of decision making. Not linear, not patriarchal, not autocratic. And leaderful in the sense that, in the sixties there was one powerful leader—Dr. King, Malcolm X—and they [were assassinated]. We share leadership in governance, we all hold that space, and it is difficult to take us out because there's so many of us—we share leadership, and that comes with accountability. . . . My mom used to say that we can't cover the sky with your hand—you need to see it for what it is. We need to, in humility, recognize that we desperately need to be working with each other in profoundly different ways and building just relationships so that we could be prepared for what's coming in front of us.[9]

UPROSE is at the forefront of leading a just climate transition. Rooted in an industrial waterfront community that bears the scars of toxic waste and extractive practices, they are successfully organizing for a local development vision that strengthens the working class character of their neighborhood while also promoting living-wage green jobs.[10] Central to their work is the commitment to leadership that centers BIPOC voices and the voices of young people. As they strive for climate justice and economic well-being, they hold themselves to serving the interests of those who have experienced marginalization. For the work to be truly effective, it must be driven by and accountable to those voices.

This model of leadership should not be new or even revolutionary for those of us who are Christians. The formation of the early church is a beautiful example of interconnected, decentralized leadership. Romans 16:1–16 mentions twenty-eight people, male and female, whom Paul names as coworkers, describing the various ways that they built up and supported this underground movement of Jesus followers that would eventually gather momentum through decades, centuries, and millennia.

Early church leaders, including Phoebe, Andronicus, and Junia, were hubs for sharing resources and information across the decentralized network. Despite persecution, this web was durable and resilient. It included wealthy homeowners sharing resources; a person whom the text describes as mothering and nurturing others in the movement; and people who risked imprisonment to teach and share this empire-challenging message of liberation and life for all people. This is a story of interconnected, hub-model leadership that is stronger than any one charismatic individual. How we tell this story matters. And it matters whom we recognize as a leader and what behaviors and actions are considered leadership. This contributes to broadening the landscape from which we draw our under-standing of leadership and who can serve.

A recent story of environmental gains—a rare bit of good news against the deluge of environmental degradation and climate chaos—is a direct result of this interconnected leader-ship model. In the 1970s, facing critical levels of deforestation, Nepal implemented a new forestry act. It handed over man-agement of national forests to community groups that oper-ated as local forest management committees. Residents near the forests now had incentive to actively manage and protect public forests and also received access to products to support their livelihoods, including fodder, fuel, and herbal medicines. Between 1996 and 2016, forest land coverage in Nepal nearly doubled, from 26 percent to 45 percent. Researchers attribute this growth to the decentralized community-led leadership model. Today, Nepal's national forests are stewarded by over twenty-two thousand community forest user groups.[11] This is good for the people, good for pangolins, red pandas, and tigers. It is good for the whole planet's carbon management and oxygen production.

No one person can change leadership cultures and sys-tems. It takes a community willing to do things differently, a community committed to building up new patterns of interac-tion. It requires significant time and focus for developing and communicating shared vision, which takes storytelling and vision-casting. One of the most hopeful things about the jour-ney of leadership in this age—of leadership in community—is that we have the opportunity to do things differently. Many things in the world are beyond our control. We can feel the forces of systems and structures acting upon us. But what is in our hands is how we choose to respond, individually and collectively. We can build microcosms of the kind of changes we want to see more broadly, ensuring that all voices are heard. Like a forest of interconnected trees, together we can build a resilient, thriving whole.

Only by moving forward with others—by recognizing and valuing our interconnectedness and building networks and coalitions of people working together to build a new way of living on the planet we call home—will we make a difference in this struggle. No individual can do that alone. This journey of seeking courageous change is work that must be done with others, though all of us have to do our own part.

6

REIMAGINING COMMUNITY

As we move toward more communal understandings of leadership, we also need to take a closer look at what exactly it is we mean by community—and why it's so essential to our future. Courageous change can only happen together, with others. We are fundamentally interconnected, and only by going deeper into community can we succeed in making the kinds of change needed to transform the future of life on this planet.

We as creatures are communal by nature. If you look at your hand under a microscope, you would see the tiny creatures of bacteria and fungi that make their home there no matter how much handwashing you do.[1] All over our bodies, inside and out, we are host to multitudes of microbes interacting, at times codependent and at other times in conflict. Science writer Ed Yong opened my eyes to the hidden world of our microbiomes in his book *I Contain Multitudes*. Yong explains, "Our lives are heavily influenced by external forces that are actually inside us, by trillions of things that are separate from us and yet very much a part of us." Physically speaking, a lot of what makes you *you* is the result of a "complex negotiation between host and microbes." And as we walking collections of microbes interact together in community, we replicate similar negotiations. Yong describes, "Every major transition in the history of life—from single-celled to multi-celled, from individuals to symbiotic collectives—has had to solve the same problem: how can the selfish interests of individuals be overcome to form cooperative groups?"[2]

The working out of community as we answer this important question is what makes us *us*. But when we approach this series of micro-struggles as nothing more than a competition, in which one person's ideas and values win over another's, we miss the potential for something greater. Embedded in our microbiomes is not only the struggle for dominance but also the potential for symbiosis: the close and long-term mutually beneficial relationship of organisms. "Symbioses," writes microbiologist David Relman, "are the ultimate examples of success through collaboration and the powerful benefits of intimate relationships."[3] Community can be a profound resource in our lives, making it possible for us to do more than we thought possible on our own.

So how do we get to symbiosis in communities that so often feel divided by conflict and struggle? Why does this sense of shared purpose seem harder for some communities to achieve than it is for others? It is time to put community under the microscope to analyze the components, to know and understand the elements, connections, and interrelationships that can lead a community to flourishing.

Community. It's a word that has so many implications and holds so much baggage. *The C-word*, we used to jokingly call it when I was at university. When I was a youth and young adult attending Mennonite churches and schools, the concept of community held so much weight as a countercultural force against the individualistic nature of Western society. The word is a world in and of itself; sometimes it seems an idol worshiped for the ideal while ignoring the reality that it entails. *For the good of the community, for the sake of the community*—these phrases are calls to humility, to interdependence, to thinking about the needs, wants, and desires of others beyond ourselves and our egos. These are good impulses in general, but there are also assumptions layered into the word: that a community is a homogenous whole. A community can be more than the sum of its parts, yet it is dangerous when individual parts are seen as less valuable than preserving the integrity of the whole. We see community at its worst when survivors of abuse are told to stay quiet because of the shame they'll bring to the group by drawing public attention. Or when the needs of some are put aside to privilege the needs of others who have more power.

And yet we dive into the messy reality of community because it is essential to a future of flourishing. There is no way forward other than finding ways to live, and work, and be together through the ups and downs of it all. Courage, perseverance, and hope are amplified and strengthened in community. One of the strengths of churches, and of other faith communities on a large and small scale, is the ability to come together to offer care, support, and mutual encouragement. When we get it right, it is a powerful place to develop patterns—of interactions, values, and practices—to lead toward that better future. Our actions matter, and the choices we make to live our values among others every day are as much a part of cultivating spirituality as is time spent in prayer or listening to sermons. When we live and work near each other, our actions shape not just our lives but our communities. We become part of building the culture around us. This is a great opportunity and a great responsibility.

Wherever we find ourselves—in classrooms, sanctuaries, meeting rooms, and in our families—we have the power to act with intention, allowing our smallest units of interaction to reflect who we want to be as a whole. These tiny elements of values, norms, and beliefs build up a larger movement and impact. Whether we're conscious of it or not, that is what we're doing with every choice and every interaction. This is magnified for people in leadership roles, including teachers in a classroom, pastors in a church, and leaders at organizations. Teachers, for example, know that students are scrutinizing every tiny thing about them. While this may feel like intense pressure—and it is!—that environment of scrutiny is part of a teacher's power to set norms in a space, to shape the nature of the classroom community. Embracing the reality that each tiny thing we do or don't do matters is key to healthy leadership. We are planting and tending seeds in hopes of a good future outcome.

My parents recently retired as business owners and a camp director and moved to a new city. Many people came forward to share what seeds my parents had planted and how they have grown. Seeds of providing structure and routine, seeds of modeling kindness in difficult customer or parent interactions, seeds of owning mistakes and working to do better. These stories, written in cards or told as anecdotes at their farewell party, were often things that my parents had totally forgotten or did not recognize as significant at the time. They couldn't have known how those seeds would bear fruit. They could not have predicted that years later, a person would express gratitude for those seeds, especially for those things that we often consider the invisible, thankless work of leadership, things like structure and accountability. But it's clear now that it's exactly because my parents understood the importance of those seeds that so much grew over the years.

This kind of power can work for good, but it can also work for evil. In graduate school, I studied how power works within civil society. Civil society can function for good or ill in building inclusion and well-being for all or in legitimizing exclusion. I studied the work of numerous theorists, including the intentionally convoluted writing of Italian political theorist Antonio Gramsci. I wrote papers and had classroom conversations full of terms like "discursive power" and "cultural hegemony." In addition to citing Gramsci, I am sure I casually referenced French social theorist Michel Foucault's ideas on how power is embedded in language and social norms much more than I had any right to. I had only a beginner's grasp of the concepts. My head was full of ideas of how power works and how to make sure it works for good and not evil.

After I completed my degree in development studies, I sought to live out these ideas in my work with nonprofits and community-based organizations and as a denominational leader in the Mennonite church. As time went on, these once-dry concepts sprang to life. Learning to think about how power works, how it is upheld, challenged, and resisted in different spaces and within groups, has given me a lens to look with intentionality at where power is held and what purpose it serves.

Any group has an opportunity to reinforce the dominant culture or challenge it through alternative patterns of interaction. Any group has the opportunity to build on values that align with Jesus' call to center the marginalized. We need to be intentional in setting up community and organizational cultures that build toward a future of flourishing in large and small ways.

When we fail, the consequences are dire. The development of the Doctrine of Discovery, and the role of white churches in justifying slavery and genocide of Indigenous Peoples, including residential schools into the late twentieth century, are significant historical examples of Gramsci's theory of hegemony. Gramsci considered civil society, the realm beyond business and government that includes churches, charities, and clubs, as the place where the values and norms that undergird the practices of institutions and systems are formed and solidified. The myriad applications of the Doctrine of Discovery demonstrate how religious institutions, and the values and beliefs promoted there, justified and upheld the actions of the European and North American governments and economic systems that subjugated Indigenous and African-origin peoples.

The other side of Gramsci's theory is that civil society organizations, including churches and faith-based organizations, have the power to challenge the status quo. They have the power to remove moral legitimacy and to offer other value systems and norms. It is no coincidence that churches played significant roles in the slavery abolition movement and the civil rights movement.

Gramsci's theory also explains the present-day links between Christian nationalism and white supremacist groups and churches—churches have a powerful ability to create and reinforce norms and values to legitimize political actions.

Churches and faith communities thus also have the power to build cultures of liberation, of belonging, of interconnection and reciprocity. And very often, they are engaged in a mix of upholding some dominant-group norms in society and challenging others. In the history of my faith tradition, I see examples of Mennonite churches both challenging and upholding the status quo. In the twentieth century, for example, North American Mennonite church structures advocated for conscientious objector status for men subject to the draft and held strong antiwar peace positions. But significantly less institutional energy and fewer resources were expended on the struggle for civil rights and racial justice,[4] and on addressing domestic violence that most often affected women.[5]

Culture-building is complex. While individual actions matter, what actually creates change is the interaction of our actions with the actions of others—the patterns and systems that are constructed and reinforced. Families have cultures. Businesses and clubs and churches have cultures. And on a larger scale, societies have cultures. Culture is another way of saying "how we do things here" and defining what is "normal." It is often like the air we breathe, ever present but rarely noticed unless something is amiss. Culture isn't static; it's constantly evolving and changing, a dynamic, kinetic relationship that changes as values, influences, and external circumstances change. In community with others, we're making "normal" together.

One of the great gifts of my life is getting to live in many cultures and subcultures, starting with my childhood move from Canada to Haiti. I've experienced how Jamaican culture is similar and different to Haitian culture, how Nepali culture is similar and different to neighboring Indian culture, and how my family's Canadian and American cultures are both similar and different. Within each of these broad categories, there are many more subcultures and variations.

Everything we learn is in relation to our first cultural context. As a child, I learned to navigate the unspoken rules and norms of my first culture, ethnically Swiss Mennonite in a British-Canadian context. Some of my inherited cultural expectations include expecting to be involved, and to have a say, both in community decisions such as in my church community and in my family. I learned to avoid the perceived loss of emotional control, to always remain pleasant and polite, even when frustrated or distressed or elated. Hard work is virtuous, especially when offered in service of others. Wealth is not something to be talked about, but you should be able to provide for yourself and your family and have enough wealth to give away as well. Be generous in donating to charity, just do it quietly and without seeking recognition.

I am still learning more about the assumptions and expectations that I carry with me. The more I'm aware of them, the more I can understand that these are not in themselves good or bad. They do not represent the right way or the wrong way to be; rather, they are part of the diversity of ways of being in the world, ways of being that I can choose to embrace or not as it fits my evolving values. And the more mindful I become of my own culture, the more I understand that there are other ways of being, other worldviews, that offer their own benefits and drawbacks.

This is especially important in justice and liberation work. During the summers of my undergraduate years, I worked for a Canadian organization involved in agriculture and cooperative development in rural Haiti. My primary qualification was that I spoke Haitian Creole, French, and English and had some experience with grant writing. They hired me to help write grants for funding from the Canadian government. I split my summer months between the organization's headquarters in Ontario and the main office and project working areas in Haiti, always with a rubric for developing outcomes and tracking indicators in hand. I loved it. Spending time chatting with colleagues over lunch in the Port-au-Prince office or, even better, in long conversations during extended visits in the rural areas, I learned from Haitian community development leaders who had been working for years to transform the situation of marginalized people. Many of my colleagues in the Haiti office had been part of the pro-democracy movement in the late 1980s and '90s, which was heavily influenced by Latin American liberation theology and theorists, including the educator and philosopher Paulo Freire.

At the root of my colleagues' development work was bringing people experiencing oppression together to reflect critically on their reality in order to transform it. *Observe, reflect, act* was the motto underlying all the project design. I don't remember when I first picked up a copy of Freire's classic book *Pedagogy of the Oppressed*, but my red paperback copy is dog-eared and full of underlined phrases. Phrases like "Liberation is a praxis: the action and reflection of men and women on their world in order to transform it."[6]

For me, liberation—my own attempts to get free from a world where my life is predicated on the suffering of others, free from the ways in which I have been steeped in and shaped by colonialism and white supremacy—requires intentional work. I seek out conversations with others who are like me and unlike me to challenge my assumptions and show me new paths forward that I haven't seen or understood before. In writing about what it looks like to transform oppression and rehumanize people whose humanity has been denied, Freire—significantly—assumes that at least some of the people reading his work are themselves from the dominant group doing the oppressing. Yes, says Freire, there is a path to allyship and co-creating a world free of exploitation, but anti-oppression work requires constant self-examination to see where ingrained biases and inherited ways of thinking are being replicated. "Those who authentically commit themselves to the people must re-examine themselves constantly," writes Freire. "[This] requires a profound rebirth. They can no longer remain as they were."[7] In relationships with others who are different from me, I come to see more clearly how my own ways of living and my actions either support liberation for all of us or work against it. It is a discipline of transformation pointing toward liberation. And it requires me to be in community, in relationship with, a diversity of people.

Community can get messy pretty quick. In my Mennonite tradition, a common response to decision-making is to say "We'll discern in community." While this points to the tradition's belief that God can and does speak through anyone, community discernment can become problematic when we don't ask ourselves whether every voice actually holds equitable weight at our table, and if not, how we might create a space where they do.

I served for two years as executive minister of Mennonite Church Eastern Canada (MCEC), the largest conference within the Canadian denomination. When I started in my role, I was tasked to develop and lead a process to determine new mission and vision statements and new strategic priorities for our regional body of about a hundred congregations across Ontario, Quebec, and New Brunswick. MCEC churches worship in over twenty languages and reflect diverse worship practices and theology within the broader Anabaptist-Mennonite tradition. Discernment in community, listening for God's leading together, is a deeply held Mennonite value. But communal discernment is never easy. And doing it well requires hearing from different voices while ensuring that no one voice or set of voices holds undue influence.

I worked closely with the conference board of directors and with talented staff colleagues. The first step was mapping out the different groups and demographics within the conference to develop a tracking framework. We wanted to make sure that our engagement strategies were aligned with all the people we needed to hear from, and this required checking in with various groups.

We named the year-long discernment process *Courageous Imagination*. One engagement strategy included a podcast series of interviews with church members of different ages and ethnicities from different locations and theological perspectives. This carefully cultivated series made it possible for people who hadn't met each other, and who may not have been likely to attend the annual church conferences, to hear from each other directly. Other engagement strategies included sharing video clips and messages on social media, hosting regional in-person gatherings, and publishing articles in our denomination's affiliated national magazine. Careful attention to the process ensured that many perspectives were heard, and that church members heard from each other directly rather than have the perspectives all filtered through the conference leadership first.

No process is perfect. We are always stumbling forward and learning as we go, but I was encouraged when congregational delegates overwhelmingly voted to adopt the new identity language and strategic priorities to guide the conference forward. I do not think this would have been possible without our intentional discernment process that sought to amplify some voices while mitigating the influence of others. This process paved the way for a shared vision of the future across a diversity of congregations.

It can be tempting to think of community as a flat structure, or with no designated structure. *We're all on the same footing, with no tiers or specialties at all.* But this just reproduces the power differentials and dynamics at play in broader society. Power is always present within a group. To exist in community well, we must learn to recognize less visible sources of power, like socioeconomic status, versus more visible sources of power, like role authority. When roles and authority are undefined, there's potential for conflict. Clarity matters. It takes moving with care and intention to set values and transparent criteria. It means setting expectations for where authority is to be held and what it is to be used for. It means planning for what will happen when disagreement and concerns surface. The structure protects the balance of the system and is set according to shared values and beliefs.

Living this new world of shared flourishing into being requires anchoring ourselves in relationships with others, building and reinforcing shared stories and shared commitment to collective values. As humans, we have a deep-seated need to belong, to find fellowship. The challenge for all of us involved in faith communities, and in other organizations and movements for justice big and small, is to bring people into relationships of belonging and purpose, to strengthen the bonds between us. These bonds will allow us to do the heavy lifting for change that must happen. Developing and articulating an understanding of our own cultures, and the culture that we want to create and uphold together, is a fundamental starting point. Critical introspection makes visible the invisible norms that form our expectations. Only then can we make conscious choices together about how decisions will be made, how conflict will be resolved, and how we'll learn from and with each other in transformative ways.

I stood in front of a u-shaped meeting table, marker in hand, listing categories like gender, education, and race on the chart paper easel. I had been invited to lead a workshop on navigating leadership transition with the board of an organization that had just hired a new female executive director after close to twenty years of male EDs in the role. I prompted the group to reflect on the characteristics that they felt gave someone's voice more or less credence around the board table. Societal power differentials like age, race, gender, and class come into play. But dynamics unique to every community influence how individual voices are valued. In this group, being a former employee or volunteer with the organization was a source of social power on the board, as was having strong personal ties to the founding churches that started the organization. Breadth and depth of relationships, comfort with speaking in front of a group, and specialized knowledge like certification in human resources or finance can also influence which voices are welcomed or listened to. When I move in North American Mennonite circles, my last name Reesor and Swiss Mennonite ethnic origins are a source of power and influence as a marker of insider status. Being White, with a formal education, and strong writing and public speaking skills, I am often able to freely share my views and influence others in group situations. In some circumstances, my (relatively) young age and female gender leave me feeling invisible. I can't count how many times people have been taken aback when they meet me and realize that I am "the boss" of the context we are in, and not a junior staff member as they first assumed upon seeing me. The changing power dynamics of different groups means that we must pay careful attention to when we need to speak up more, and when we should take a step back to create more space for other voices to be heard.

It's not that power is bad in and of itself. Power simply means how things happen, what gets done, and what it takes for it to happen. Using similar exercises to reflect on the unique dynamics of any group, such as a board or church council, allows us to be intentional about hearing all the diverse perspectives around the table. Reflecting on group dynamics helps us attune to when sources of power are privileging some voices over others.

If we believe that God can and does speak through anyone, not just designated priests or leaders, we have to make sure we are listening to all the voices at our table, and thinking about who is not at the table. Otherwise we might miss what God has to say. And if the Bible tells us anything about how God speaks and acts, it is that God is often active on the margins, in unexpected ways and with unexpected people. The women who went to attend to Jesus' body at the tomb—Mary Magdalene, Joanna, Mary the mother of James, and others— were first to hear the news of Jesus' resurrection but were not believed by the others, including Jesus' inner circle of eleven disciples (Luke 24). The women had a revelation, they had news that changed everything, but their companions did not believe them. What better example of why we need to listen to each other, and believe each other, in community.

Many pressures call us away from community. In North America, the dominant culture emphasizes the success and comfort of the individual instead of the collective. Reorienting toward a more collective way of being in community together with others can feel like swimming upstream. Many of us face economic pressures: the time and emotional energy we have for volunteering and community organizing is affected by the need to earn an income and care for our children, families, and households. And yet community is also survival—the deeper the bonds and connections we have to our neighbors and others, the more resilient we can be when it comes to asking for and to giving help. Part of the important work of culture-building in community is reinforcing the idea that we do in fact need each other. We need places and spaces of belonging and connection, of reliance on each other.

Community is emergent; like bacteria, it can be cultivated and tended, possibly tamed or squashed, but not fully controlled in its outcomes. It's about the conditions we create and the life that can flourish. Building cultures of liberation and flourishing, cultures where many voices matter and can be heard, is a way of tending the soil from which the seeds of change can sprout and grow.

7

REIMAGINING ACCOUNTABILITY AND REPAIRING HARM

Given the desperate state of our climate, every solution is on the table. Things cannot continue as they are without risking catastrophic loss. Scientists are testing everything they can think of to reduce the warming effects of carbon emissions in the earth's atmosphere. There is no way around reducing fossil fuels emissions in the long term, but researchers are exploring every possible option to buy more time to transition away from fossil fuels and to mitigate catastrophic impact from our warming climate. One idea is to shoot particulate materials into the atmosphere, imitating the effect of the lingering ash from a volcano, which we know can have a cooling effect.

I once started writing a novel set in a distant future in which global powers are debating whether to use a technology like this, one that would halt global warming but also turn the whole sky grey and forever block the view of the stars from Earth. In my story, everyday people are taking sides about whether to trust a technological fix that might work and yet might have unintended consequences, like disrupting bird migration. Wary of the technology, "Earthers" think humans have no right messing with the climate and taking such risks. They believe that only the slow work of changing lifestyles and consumption patterns can move humanity, and the non-human world, forward to a livable future.

As I thought through this plotline, I polled friends and family on what side they would take in this hypothetical future. Some sided with the new technology, feeling that it is already too late and we urgently need any and all solutions that might keep our polar ice caps from fully melting and hold the chaos of climate breakdown at bay. The cost of inaction already outweighs any potential unintended side effects, some argued. Others felt that without addressing the reasons we got into this mess in the first place—the inequalities and overconsumption and exploitation of people and natural resources—no technological fix will make a long-term difference. The pattern of harm to people and to the earth will continue. As I talked with my friends and family members, one thing became clear. This is not a hypothetical debate for one hundred years in the future. This is where we are today. And the debate about technical solutions for the climate crisis is really a debate about change. How much change can our global economic and social systems make, and how fast? How much change are global leaders willing to make so that a better future is possible?

Research into possible warming reduction techniques is ongoing at Harvard University's Solar Geoengineering Research Program, where physical scientists, social scientists, and philosophers are actively studying technologies to change the physical environment and either deflect some sunlight away from Earth or increase how much solar radiation can escape back into space and out of the atmosphere. This could perhaps be achieved by thinning cirrus clouds so that less heat is trapped near the earth. Another branch of the program's research, marine cloud brightening, studies modifying clouds over the ocean so that they better reflect sunlight away from the earth. Yet another technology, called stratospheric aerosol scattering, replicates the cooling action of volcanic ash by shooting sparkly bits of particulate into the upper atmosphere to deflect sunlight away from the earth, thus contributing to a small cooling effect. These technologies cannot be a substitute for reducing carbon emissions, but at their best, they may buy us some time.[1]

In the case of all these technologies, we just don't know how intervening would change the weather, and what regional variations might occur. But the even murkier question is one of ethics: Is it ethically acceptable to have some parts of the earth experience lower amounts of sunlight, and thus potentially harm some ecosystems and the people who depend on them? How will we decide what risks are acceptable and who is expected to bear the brunt of the vulnerability to the risks? Whose voice will count in evaluating whether an intervention is acceptable or if the cost is too high? Is it worth spending time and money to research and potentially implement these short-term fixes when the money could be spent working on what we know works: reducing the use of fossil fuels and moving toward a just energy transition globally?

These questions are inescapably political. Philosopher Britta Clark notes that the arguments both for and against solar geoengineering make assumptions about political conditions and what political actors, like national governments and UN bodies, can be reasonably expected to do in the present and near future. At this point, funding for solar geoengineering research comes from a handful of high-income, high-carbon-emitting countries, led by the United States. If this technology is to have any role in climate change mitigation in the next decade, it will need an immediate, rapid increase in funding. And the focus of the question right now is whether it is something to invest time, money, and brain power into, or whether that resource focus should be directed at what we know works—moving toward a just energy transition as rapidly as possible. There is a very real risk in the alluring promise of a "fix" that requires no change in the status quo—and which would almost certainly be the result of solutions funded by the richest nations in the world. It could just allow more feet-dragging and obfuscation by fossil fuel interests, further delaying the shift away from fossil fuels that must happen as soon as possible.[2]

Like the young adult protagonists I imagined in the draft of my novel, I am an Earther. I see the path forward as one that requires us first to go deep into history to understand the factors that got us here. It requires being accountable, by which I mean taking responsibility for harm done. And it requires undertaking repair toward making things right. What I see in the allure of a promised quick fix like solar geoengineering is an attempt to duck responsibility for harm done to the environment and to people over centuries of exploitation. I see an excuse to go on with the same practices that got us here.

Attempts at accountability and repair are already happening on a global scale, through the UN Conference on Climate Change and associated global summits on climate change, called the Conference of the Parties, or COP. At the conclusion of COP27 in November 2022, countries agreed to set up the Loss and Damage Fund as a way for wealthy, high-carbon-emitting nations to fund the most vulnerable, highly affected nations that have contributed only a fraction of the emissions that led us here.[3] It is an achievement that the fund exists at all, and that wealthy countries are beginning to make financial commitments to fund it (though committing funds and actually paying them are not the same thing). All of this requires political will more than technical prowess. For a democratic country like Canada, it means getting Canadians on board with tax dollars being spent in this way. It requires culture work to understand and value accountability, moral responsibility, and repair or reparations for harm done. This is nearly impossible to do at the level of international relations if we aren't practicing it on smaller scales to build and strengthen these cultural values.

Like adrienne maree brown, I think that fractals are a useful metaphor for building movements that are consistent from the smallest components to the largest.[4] Building broad cultural values of accountability and repair means that we have to start practicing accountability and repair. This happens from the small units of our relationships with our families, neighbors, and coworkers all the way through to our larger identity groups, institutions, and nations. It means practicing new ways of being and seeing ourselves in relationship to others, and in our interconnected relationship to the broader natural world.

Community, as we have seen, is messy. We're always falling short of our good intentions. And there are even more challenges to navigate when serious harm occurs. How we respond when this happens is key to building a culture of accountability and repair. We've got to find ways to expand our capacity to hold discomfort, to deal with conflict constructively in groups, movements, churches, organizations. It's not a distraction; it's the core of our work.

Perfectionism, roughly defined as "a combination of excessively high personal standards and overly critical self-evaluations," has been on the rise over the past decades. A study of British, American, and Canadian college students between 1989 and 2016 found that "recent generations of young people perceive that others are more demanding of them, are more demanding of others, and are more demanding of themselves." The study authors note that these years of increasing perfectionism correspond with the rise of neoliberal forms of government in these same countries that have "emphasized competitive individualism."[5] Our cultural values trickle down, shaping how we see ourselves and our individual actions. When we believe we must be perfect, any critique can feel threatening. And these rising perfectionist tendencies make it difficult to give and receive feedback well.

If we are serious about transforming cultural values of individualism, perfectionism, and competition into cultural values of collective responsibility, of accountability and repair, we face a big challenge. We must find a way to make it psychologically safe enough for accountability and repair to happen. This means releasing some of the expectations we place on ourselves and on others, and recognizing the unequal tolerance we sometimes feel for the real and perceived shortcomings of others. Throw in challenges to the status quo as changing norms make space for women and minorities to take more visible leadership roles, with resulting loss of power for some as others gain more power in society, and it's a tinderbox waiting for a spark to explode into conflict.

One of the best leadership trainings I've attended included a session on how to receive feedback. We need to practice receiving feedback as much as, if not more than, we need to practice giving it. So often, we worry about how to tell others exactly what is wrong with their actions in a way that will get our point across but not ruffle feathers. Or on our worst days, we feel justified in giving someone a piece of our mind that will really teach them a lesson (we think!). This training flipped that on its head; my top priority now is not getting better at delivering feedback effectively but getting better at receiving it nondefensively. This means considering what I can learn from the feedback and choosing whether I believe the feedback is relevant to me or says more about the person giving it. Working on receptiveness has also helped me consider how to give feedback in ways that help others to be receptive as well, though I am continually learning that I cannot directly control how others experience my feedback.

Getting better at receiving feedback is another way to think about getting better at accepting accountability. We have all seen examples of what accountability is not. I have a few in my family history. I once heard the story of how my great-grandfather Orla Heise was reprimanded by the church leadership because his house and farm homestead were too fancy. Orla was part of the Brethren in Christ Anabaptist group that also settled in the Markham area around the same time as my Reesor ancestors. Orla may have been guilty of the sin of pride in keeping things beyond just the expected modest *spic, span, and tidy.* I have trouble imagining just how fancy this farming family's homestead must have been, and in what ways, for it to get called out for being "too much." Carved curlicues on the porch rails of the brick farmhouse? Brightly colored paint trim? A snazzy weathervane on the barn? Excessively lovely flower gardens? It was probably the flowers. I've been told that Orla's wife, my great-grandmother Catherine, loved flowers, so much that Orla raised it at a church council meeting, putting forward a motion that flowers should be allowed in the church as decorations. It didn't pass, but reportedly, Orla was not discouraged. "No matter, it'll pass next year," he is remembered as saying.

For the record, I'm certain that no one will ever accuse me of having too much pride for my house and yard, though I do admit to being excessively proud of my peonies. The only time I've experienced a reprimand for how my house and yard look is when someone complained to the city bylaw officers about the height and shagginess of the hedge around our yard. We were forced to cut it back.

The family story, one I'm not even sure actually happened, about the Heise homestead being too fancy is about excessive accountability, more related to cementing power and control through uniformity than addressing any ills. It is unclear what harm there was in the self-expression of the Heise family. In contrast, our overgrown hedge limited traffic and pedestrian visibility near our corner lot, so fair enough, we should have kept it trimmed lower. It was a reasonable call to accountability for us, reminding us that our laidback approach to shrubbery maintenance had a negative impact on others around us. I wish, though, that whoever made the complaint had talked to us before calling the city, because we would have happily accepted the reminder to trim it down. Instead, we were left with unanswered questions. Was it the appearance that bothered them? Had they had a scary experience with traffic because the hedge blocked their view? Was the problem actually the new treehouse that we had built in a tree right at the corner of the yard, bordering the hedge?

Not knowing who complained or what prompted it made us feel singled out and suspicious of our neighbors. It is possible that the person who made the complaint did not feel safe initiating a conversation, especially if they didn't know us personally. They couldn't know how we might react, if we would say or do something threatening or retaliate in some way. I can't say that they did the wrong thing by calling the city instead of talking to us directly. But I wish they had started with a conversation. I wish we could have addressed it relationally instead of through a punitive administrative process.

A conversation with a real person who was affected by our hedge may have been uncomfortable, but I hope that it would have led to the possibility of a changed relationship. Starting with a conversation, starting with curiosity and a willingness to hear different perspectives, listening for the unmet needs under the surface—this is how I handle conflict at my best. Though getting up my courage to step into these kinds of conflict is always a challenge, no matter my conviction that the conversations matter.

I come from a culture that often fears conflict. Any sign of visible, outward disagreement is interpreted as a sign of failure and the breakdown of harmony. Conflict resolution, then, becomes about returning to peace, returning to harmony. My own journey of transformation is coming to understand that conflict is not a sign of communication failure, or lack of respectful and polite interaction, though of course respectful and dignified behavior and speech is what I believe we all owe to each other. I am coming to understand, trying to move from head knowledge to heart knowledge, that conflict can be generative and that it is an essential part of giving and receiving accountability to each other for the impact of our actions. By that, I mean that conflict can open up new possibilities and push us beyond our limited perspectives to deeper empathy. Only when we encounter someone else's perspective in opposition to our own can we really, truly consider the value of each other and understand where another person is coming from. The more that I can tend to my shame and conflict-triggered perfectionism, the more I can remain open and growth-oriented, the more I am able to be receptive to this creative power of conflict. It is not comfortable, and I don't think it ever will be. If it feels comfortable, it is unlikely that we are taking seriously the personal impacts of whatever brings us into clashes of needs, wants, and goals. Comfort isn't—or shouldn't be—our primary goal.

My work with my church conference, Mennonite Church Eastern Canada, included addressing historical matters of clergy abuse. As I navigated this difficult terrain, the best advice I received was from Anabaptist theologian and survivor advocate Carol Penner. There will always be conflict in faith communities after abuse comes to light, she shared. Not everyone will agree on the best ways to respond. That advice was liberating; it normalized conflict in accountability processes instead of seeing conflict as a sign of leadership failure. Conflict is inevitable. There are many perspectives and experiences, many conflicting needs, wants, and desires, even in a context where everyone agrees that abuse should not happen. That truth freed me from trying to manage conflict. Instead, I could focus on whoever was most vulnerable in a specific situation, and on what steps could bring safety and a move toward healing for survivors.

For a leader with power to act or not to act, to avoid conflict is to avoid accountability. Stepping into responsibility means stepping into conflict and understanding that each step you take or don't take will harm someone in one way or another. It comes down to choices guided by values, as well as the humility to be willing to get it wrong yet offer yourself in service anyway. Leaders must seek to get it right, not to be right.

For leaders—whether government leaders determining the ethics of investing in solar geoengineering research, countries opting to contribute to the global Loss and Damage Fund for climate change mitigation, or church leaders addressing harm in a congregation—each step will have consequences and impacts on different people in different ways. Each step, each choice, ripples out. The higher-stakes the decision, the greater the pushback. The nature of leadership is to be accountable for choices, as each of us ought to be as we walk through the world and act in whatever space is available to us. There is no neutral path. Leading means setting your values and taking each step in accordance with those values, knowing that there will be ripples and waves and backwash with each action taken or not. If you're not making waves, then perhaps you are not living into the responsibilities of the role. Sometimes all you can do is lean on your values and discern the least bad option in any given situation. There will be ripples and consequences of any and every action or inaction. What matters is stepping into the stream anyway and letting it flow around you as best you can, moving toward wholeness and restoration that focuses on the most vulnerable.

When we truly engage the perspectives of others, especially those with less power than us, we may be asked to give up our privilege on the path toward wholeness and restoration for the most vulnerable. Or that privilege may even be taken from us on the journey to move from social hierarchies to a more equitable sharing of power in a community, organization, or society. The loss of privilege can sometimes feel like harm. For those of us who are used to having our voice be heard louder than others, to experience less influence can feel like we are not valued anymore. To be decentered, to have less influence than we expected, can feel like harm or like "bad leadership" that is not listening well to what you say.

As we explored in the earlier chapter on leadership, when women and minorities are in leadership roles, they are more likely to have their leadership questioned and undermined. They are likely to encounter greater scrutiny than leaders who are White or male. When women and minorities in leadership challenge established hierarchies of power, they are most prone to criticism and pushback. This can take the form of weaponizing accountability practices in order to return to how things were in the imagined better past. In organizational or church cultures where conflict signals failure, the pressure to address this "bad leadership" that is causing conflict and return to harmony maintains the status quo, which means that underrepresented and more marginalized voices are blocked from enacting change.

Change and conflict go hand in hand. It's not that harmony is a bad goal or state to be in. Rather, the pursuit of harmony at the cost of silencing dissent and reform works against the goal of listening to many voices and being willing to turn the tables of power. For me, it comes back to the multidimensional analysis of power and a biblical ethic of siding with the most marginalized or vulnerable in any given situation. It is critical to keep this power lens in view during conflicts, because any challenge to the power distribution of the status quo will create conflict. To make courageous changes in our churches, in our communities, in our world, there will need to be conflict. And conflict, uncomfortable as it may be, is not the same as harm. We won't always agree on the best way forward to repair situations of harm, and we won't even agree on what actions need accountability and repair. But I hope that all of us keep actively seeking out and strengthening our humility muscles to be open to hearing about the impact of our actions so that we can consider possibilities for moving beyond that can lead to flourishing for all. It takes a community to build these values and practices into a culture that cares about understanding and acting on harm.

Accountability and repair of harm is a practice for individuals to work on in communities, and it is a practice for communities and societies to engage together for the flourishing of our communities. When we practice accountability on the small scale, between each other as individuals, in families, in workplaces and movements together, it strengthens our emotional capacity and resilience to undertake larger-scale reparations and make things right. Nobel Peace Laureate Desmond Tutu writes in his book on the South African Truth and Reconciliation Commission that "to work for reconciliation is to want to realize God's dream for humanity—when we will know that we are indeed members of one family, bound together in a delicate network of interdependence."[6] The TRC was an innovative accountability and reconciliation process that sought to address the violence and human rights abuses of South African apartheid. As Tutu writes, part of moving forward together is working to strengthen this network of interdependence, building momentum to fuel systemic and political decision-making that can embed into a society the acknowledgment of harm and steps toward repair in a lasting way.

My favorite Bible story of repentance—of repair of harm in action—is the story of Zacchaeus, found in Luke 19:1–10.

The writer of the gospel of Luke tells us that Zacchaeus is a tax official who likely earned his wealth through corruption and by exploiting people. When Zacchaeus encounters Jesus and experiences unconditional welcome, he is moved to turn around his life, to repent and go in another direction. Without being asked, Zacchaeus takes it upon himself to try to make it right in material ways, not just with an apology or confession of wrongdoing. Zacchaeus even says he will repay not just all that he cheated people out of, but four times the amount, recognizing and repairing the wrongdoing and hardship he caused. We don't know what transformation is already under-way in Zacchaeus's heart as he climbs a tree to catch a glimpse of Jesus. But in that window of time between Jesus inviting himself over for dinner at Zacchaeus's house and Zacchaeus's actually hosting the meal, the tax official acknowledges that he has done wrong, that he has hurt people, and that he wants to go down a path toward making things right—a path to restitution and reparation. Zacchaeus doesn't wait to be told exactly what he needs to do to make things right or ask how much (or how little) would be enough. It is as if scales fall from his eyes and he sees exactly what he wants to do. He sees the kind of person he wants to be in relation to those around him and assesses what it will take.

Many of us are, in our own ways, Zacchaeus. His story is one of an individual awakening to his role in the legacy of harm, of colonialism and exploitation; over the centuries, this same legacy has led us to where we are in the Anthropo-cene. The actions of just one person can't undo that alone, though each of us has a part to play. As we have seen already, our individual actions help build a culture; when we respond like Zacchaeus, we model the kind of culture—the culture of accountability and repair—we'd like to create.

In my own life, as a citizen of a country built on the primary act of theft of land and cultural genocide of Indigenous Peoples, my major learnings on confession, repentance, and repair come from Canada's Truth and Reconciliation Commission. After years of studying the historical record and hearing the stories from survivors of the abusive treatment that generations of Indigenous children were subjected to in Canada's residential school system, the Canadian commission issued its final report in 2015.[7]

The TRC in Canada was foundational in making churches in particular come face-to-face with the harm of church-run residential schools. My own denomination, Mennonite Church Canada, did not have official agreements to run residential schools on behalf of the government like larger denominations did, but the TRC provided significant motivation for our European-origin churches to consider the harm of cultural genocide that we participated in through what was understood at the time to be "doing good"—adopting Indigenous children into White families in the so-called Sixties Scoop and supporting Mennonite-affiliated day schools and residential schools that understood themselves to be engaged in spiritual warfare against Indigenous spiritualities and cultural practices.[8] Years after the TRC, we are now in a new moment marked by the recovery of mass graves of children at former residential school sites. We see even more clearly that the truth-telling must continue, until the magnitude of the harm—the nooks and crannies, the workings of it—becomes clear, the truth permeating our skin until it transforms us to see with new eyes and walk forward in new ways. The goal is not that we would be weighted down in guilt, though there is guilt and shame aplenty to experience along the way. Walking this path of repentance and sitting with the knowledge of harm—allowing ourselves to sit with that guilt as it moves us to acts of repentance and repair—is the gateway to transformation, to opening the door to change our current state into a different kind of future going forward. To learn, and then in learning to do better and take steps toward repair.

In my church congregation, it's been a slow journey, one of fits and starts, to begin to walk the path of repentance and reparations toward Indigenous Peoples. A land acknowledgment displayed on a plaque affixed to the church building reminds us as we walk into the building of the First Nations that have been caretakers of this land for untold generations, and of the promises made but not honored. As a congregation, we've donated funds to Crow Shield Lodge, an Indigenous organization in our community that focuses on land-based healing and reconciliation, drawing on Indigenous spiritual and cultural practices.

Crow Shield Lodge founder and Chapleau Creek Cree Nation member Clarence Cachagee and Russian Mennonite-origin writer Seth Ratzlaff, in their book *North Wind Man*, remind us that we are all on a healing journey. "We believe that careful attention to history's injustices and ongoing harm opens future pathways to accountability, healing and reconciliation," they write. "We believe these truths are relevant to all of us, because everyone is on a healing journey, whether acknowledged or not."[9] There is no arriving at the destination of reconciliation; what matters is committing to the journey. And just as a life of faith, or a marriage, requires recommitting ourselves over and over again, so must we continually recommit to the journey of repentance and repair.

Our planet bears unmistakable scars and faces ongoing harm because of unsustainable resource extraction and climate change. We need to build a culture together of accountability and repair, with openness to learning and growing. Stepping into that vision, that intention for what repair to people and to the environment could look like, is a journey of accountability, a journey of humility. There is no quick fix, no way to sidestep what caused the harm in the first place.

For those like me who are descended from and a citizen of a settler-origin country and culture, this calls for setting aside perfectionism and defensiveness, rejecting apathy, and cultivating new awareness of interdependence and connection. As we do so, we step into relationships of reparation and repair that can point the way to a future where flourishing for all people is possible. Like Zacchaeus, we need our discomfort with the knowledge of having caused harm to push us not to run away from community, but to seek out ways to practice repair and restitution. And that takes courage. There is little glory to be had in stepping into our responsibilities to each other and to the world around us. Courageous change is not for the fickle. It takes courage to be willing to turn around, to go another direction and act to repair what was damaged. Sometimes the loss is irreplaceable. But when we get this right, when we build up a culture of accountability and repair, as individuals in our relationships with each other and as churches, as communities, and as nations, it opens the path for new possibilities.

8

REIMAGINING CHURCH AS MOVEMENT

I started going to church because I was born into it. My family went, so I went too. But I've remained connected to the Christian faith tradition after all these years because it is a place where the streams of interdependence, of community and culture-building, of storytelling to shape values of flourishing, can converge into something beautiful, something that links us to past and future and can sustain us in hard times.

On the farm where I grew up, there is an irrigation pond. In the spring, as snow melts, streams of water collect off the fields. The rivulets carve courses through the reeds and cattails at the edge and then gather into the pond, filling it with water that will be used for watering strawberries, peas, and beans in the hot, dry months of the summer growing season. Throughout the year, the pond also draws in herons, muskrats, and frogs. All kinds of life congregates here and is nourished.

I like to think of the streams of stories, beliefs, and practices that we've been exploring in this book as converging in the pond of church, a life-giving source of strength for the changes needed to move toward a flourishing future for people and for the planet. Church—as a space, as a body, as a movement that encompasses all kinds of ways that people organize themselves together—can be a place where these ideas and shifts come together to be lived out into the world.

But these values and culture shifts also reorient *how* we think of church. What do we need church to be, and to become, as we find our way forward together? What would courageous change look like for the church? The status quo has gotten us here. The challenges facing us require expanding our imaginations of what it means to be the church from a set of fixed institutions to a fluid and agile movement connecting groups and individuals together. In the years that I lived on the farm, I saw the pond grow, change and evolve as trees grew around the edges, cattails took hold, and the marshy areas at its edges were allowed to grow wild. From redwing blackbirds to frogs to water striders, as the human-made pond went through a process of revitalization and the plant, animal, and insect life flourished. Can church be as beautiful and surprising and life-giving as an irrigation pond that evolves into a flourishing wetland?

Looking at the challenges of this time, at the scope and scale of what kind of changes are needed as we live in the Anthropocene and seek futures of life and liberation from experiencing and causing oppression, it is clear that we need each other. We need each other to tell and retell stories about ourselves and our place in the world and the cosmos that lead to values of interconnection, reciprocity, and mutual flourishing. We need media, educational resources, and art that tell a different story about the place of humans in the cosmos, one in which people are interconnected in creation, part of it but not the center. We need places to practice thinking and acting beyond hierarchy and binaries to embodied interdependence. Faith communities, including churches in all shapes and sizes, can be transformative in the climate crisis, serving as sites of cultural value change to enable the widespread social change necessary to move away from a value system of hierarchy, domination, and extraction to value systems centered on the interdependent thriving of all.

As Christians, this is in our very DNA. As we learned in chapter 3 from Julian Guamán, an Indigenous Kichwa Mennonite author and church leader from the Ecuadorian Andes, to exist is to be in community: to be in reciprocal relationship with people and with the natural world. Understanding oneself as having a responsibility to other people and to the natural world, to exist in community, and to practice reconciliation—making things right and bringing relationships into harmony again—is a practice of lived discipleship, of following Jesus and a way of life that has tangible implications. Life is precious and rare. How are we organizing to protect it? How can we protect the flourishing of people and the world we are interconnected in and depend on?

If I've learned anything about the nature of God from reading the Bible, it is that God is often found on the margins, working in unexpected ways. The midwives Shiphrah and Puah resisted Pharaoh's genocide against the Hebrews. Mary sang of upside-down power and hope amid hardship and despair. And the early church brought people from all social backgrounds and status levels together as siblings in building up the movement of Jesus followers. Healing, renewing, restoring, dwelling in and with people experiencing oppression—these hallmarks of divine presence cannot be contained. I saw this in my childhood church experiences in Haiti, where faith stories of God's deliverance and the community of believers was a source of strength and courage for people experiencing political repression. And I've seen it in my community today, including at the interfaith prayer vigil for climate justice on a chilly November night. We come together to be sustained in hope, to care for each other, and to be inspired to act for justice.

In the history of my own faith tradition, renewal and emergence have come from movements. Jesus called, taught, and sent out disciples. The community that developed around his teachings lived out an upside-down social order. The early church began with house churches and gatherings of believers, ideas, and encouragements shared in letters carried by ship across borders and seas. The Anabaptist movement that emerged in the 1500s began outside the bounds of the institutional, state-affiliated church. Like the early church, it built capacity and spread through underground networks, forest gatherings, and house churches, through revolutionary sewing circles and conversations in marketplaces and workshops. These movements were powered by relationships, by hospitality, by expressions of care and the sharing of wisdom and teachings in both formal and informal ways. They offered community, belonging, and dignity to people from many socioeconomic backgrounds, and they integrated values and daily lived actions. And they emerged with a wide, decentralized base of leadership that allowed flexibility and adaptation.

The emergent, communal nature of these movements were at the forefront of my mind as I accepted the call to denominational leadership within the Mennonite church. It was September 2020. In the heart of pandemic turbulence, my installation service happened on Zoom. I stood at the front of a mostly empty church building and addressed the camera that was livestreaming the service. "We are the people of Mennonite Church Eastern Canada, of Mennonite Church Canada, of the global Anabaptist family of Mennonite World Conference, and part of the body of God's church through the ages," I said.

> We are not here to be an institution; we are a spiritual movement together, seeking to follow Jesus in life and put our faith into action. We are a movement that builds up communities of healing and hope, sharing God's love out in a hurting world. We are a movement that is rooted in the deep joy and love that comes from knowing that we, and all human beings, are created good, in God's image. We are a movement that says we must seek out and care for the vulnerable among us. We welcome strangers, we lift up the lowly, and we live in hope for God's great shalom, where there is wholeness, justice and peace for all. We are a movement that is both ancient and new, drawing on Scripture and seeking to follow the Spirit's leading in our lives today.[1]

It mattered to me to share a vision for MCEC as a movement. This body of congregations that worships in over twenty languages, that has a diversity of beliefs and worship practices within the broader Anabaptist-Mennonite tradition, at times has more that divides it than unites it. Our movement is also connected to church-affiliated schools, camps, and a broader set of organizations and institutions, along with the many individual church members and those who serve as pastors, leaders, and staff. In collaboration with a peace research center, we attempted to map the relationships and connections between the various actors in this ecosystem, and found a rich web that went well beyond the member congregations to other community agencies and organizations.[2] That web of relationships, that macro view of the movement of our church conference, is a truer image of the whole than the idea of MCEC as a singular regional church institution. Movements have space for difference, for people and organizations to join with different but overlapping priorities. They can ebb and flow and blur into other movements around the edges. And they are bigger than any one part or institution.[3]

Institutions are not bad in and of themselves. At their core, institutions, and the larger structures and systems that they make up, are vehicles for organizing people and resources to achieve specific purposes. But it seems to me that when we think about the church, we conflate certain ways of organizing people and resources together with the larger purpose of being the body of Christ in the world. Movements bring institutions, different kinds of organizations and individuals into community for a shared purpose. The existence of a specific organization or institution within a larger movement is less important than the broader movement itself, which will shift and flow over time in different ways.

Courageous change asks us to imagine not what exists but what could and should. Kelly Hayes and Mariame Kaba, drawing on their experience as community organizers and social justice activists, write: "Transformative change happens when we are willing to build the things we know must exist."[4] Imagine if we thought about church this way. Not church as a specific set of organizations that must be upheld, strengthened, and protected, but church as the collection of spaces and places that provide a home for love, compassion, hope, interconnection, and experiences of the divine, a place where the sacred nature of life will be nurtured. A place to tell the stories, new and old, that ground us in this time and place and help us imagine the future that could be, the future where the lion lies down with the lamb and people are at peace. Peace with people, peace with nature, peace with the divine who dwells among us in the known and unknown matter of the universe and who fills the intermolecular space between all the particles of creation. A shalom of the cosmos.

It is no secret that church-as-usual is changing in North America. Census data across the United States and Canada shows declining denominational affiliation. This matches the experience of many congregations who are living the reality; many churches find that fewer people are actively taking part, and younger generations in particular are less and less present in institutional church spaces. Between 2001 and 2021, the percentage of people who identified as Christian in Canada dropped from nearly 80 percent to just above 50 percent. Among young adults, the percentage is even lower; only a third of Canadians between the ages of twenty-five and thirty-four identified as Christian.[5] In the United States, a study found that between 2019 and 2022 the number of people who reported that they seldom or never visit religious services increased from 45 percent to 57 percent.[6]

A 2022 report prepared by Mennonite Church Canada delegates to the Mennonite World Conference Global Youth Summit offers insight into young adult disengagement. The report authors surveyed youth and young adults across Canada and identified four key themes. First, many youth and young adults reported that they do not feel a sense of belonging at church, so they seek community and answers to faith questions elsewhere. Second, they did not feel heard in church. For those who have stayed in congregations, many "expressed feelings of neglect, lack of attention from church communities, and do not experience their spiritual lives being nurtured." Young adults in church leadership felt pressured to meet others' expectations, and often felt that their concerns were not addressed. Third, respondents said they see the church wrestling with an identity crisis as it deals with a legacy of oppression and harm committed in the name of Christianity. The report noted that respondents "have experienced and witnessed many types of oppression, judgment, and lack of acceptance toward those seen as not part of the church." It was hard for them to stay in a church that does not seem to be acting in Christlike ways. Finally, those surveyed believed that the church must find ways to meaningfully engage with and address the many contemporary challenges of social, political, economic, and environmental issues. The study authors, young adults themselves, found that young adults are yearning to experience belonging and connection, to have places to grow and be strengthened in their faith, and to meaningfully engage with the challenges of our world. And they are finding other places and spaces to do that when those needs are not being met in traditional congregational life.[7]

The documentary *gOD-Talk: A Black Millennials and Faith Conversation* explores a Pew research study of Black youth and religion in the United States. For Black young adults born between 1981 and 1996, even as fewer identified as Christian by specific religious affiliation, the vast majority—over 96 percent—still expressed belief in God or a higher power. "They're not walking away from the belief in something greater than themselves," said film creator and producer Teddy Reeves. "They're walking away from institutions. And so that, for us, is something for us to begin to grapple with as we think about the longevity and sustainability of our religious institutions in this country."[8]

Envisioning church differently will require courageous imagination as we think beyond reforming today's church institutions and organizations to the scale of developing new paradigms—new ways of seeing and inhabiting the world around us. The retelling chapters of this book explore how the values and beliefs and the origin stories that we inherited have contributed to the dominant colonial worldview, one of hierarchies and divisions, of extraction and exploitation of people and of natural resources. Only when we open our eyes to ways this worldview has shaped us—when we can learn to name the very air we breathe—can we see other ways of being, other possibilities for existing in the world, other paradigms that can lead to outcomes of flourishing that don't rely on the oppression of others.

Decolonization is one way to frame this journey of learning and change. Scholars from the Gesturing Towards Decolonial Futures Collective offer a model for thinking about how to move from the colonial patterns of relationship that reproduce existing power differences and struggles to new imaginings for a radically different foundation of belief and actions. The phrase "gesturing towards decolonial futures" expresses that we can only *hope* to move in this direction, because we are always embedded in the current reality. In this space of reforming institutions and systems, the emphasis is on changing the rules and functioning of current structures to address how they have led some to be excluded. This includes, for example, reforming organizations and systems to address patriarchy and racism to ensure more equitable access to the resources in the system. In the space that the authors term "beyond-reform," the emphasis is on moving toward different worldviews, imagining different ways of knowing and being.[9]

Anyone who has ever led or worked or functioned within an institution knows how easy it is to become exhausted by these daily internal battles. I'm not saying that these struggles aren't important—they are. Without women in ministry before me struggling to change the theology and policies, as well as the cultural acceptance for women to hold spiritual leadership roles, I would not have been appointed as executive minister of my church conference. Others have and are struggling to make space for LGBTQ2S+ clergy, and for leadership representation that matches the demographics of the member congregations, addressing the White-dominant leadership culture across my Mennonite denomination. These choices, the struggles over who will have a voice and what criteria will drive decision-making, have real implications for people's lives, and it is naive to think that we can fully separate ourselves from those struggles for voice, agency, and power.

But important as they are, these reforms alone cannot be the means of transformation into something beyond. In my life and career, I feel constantly pulled between the role of reformer—trying to remake and adapt historic institutions to be relevant to the present and emerging context—and of moving beyond those zero-sum power struggles to the place of dreaming, imagining, living in a new way. Of making new spaces and places for liberation and flourishing. Geographer and abolition activist Ruth Wilson Gilmore tells us that freedom is a place, and we make it:

> "Freedom is a place" means we combine resources, ingenuity, and commitment to produce the conditions in which life is precious for all. . . . So, no matter the struggle, freedom is happening somewhere. Through different forces and relations to power, the people are constantly figuring

out how to shift, how to build, how to consolidate the capacity for people to flourish, to mobilize our communities, and stay in motion until satisfied.[10]

As I do this work of imagining, I've been co-creating a network of Anabaptist-connected scholars and faith leaders who exist on the margins in some way and who have a longing for what church could become—and sometimes is—but is mostly not yet. We call ourselves the Junia Centre, a reference to the apostle Junia, who was misgendered as male for centuries, in recognition that some voices have been silenced or stifled in the work of the church over the millennia and today. As we think together about what it means for us, a group of people representing different ages, ethnicities, genders, and sexualities, to come together, we recognize that part of the work is simply existing. Just claiming space in the world, with our multiple identities and shared belief that a more inclusive, richer, interconnected way of being in the faith is possible, is one way we are imagining something different.

The unchanging constancy of God is love—the inherent belovedness of all people, all creation, pronounced good at the very moment of being. This love is a life force. It is the generative power of possibility, of new life, of regrowth and repair. It is the divine power of flourishing on the margins, in the cracks, in the unexpected places. And so our faith-inspired movements, including churches and other organizations that make up the movement ecosystem, must also exude this organizing, growing, building nature, following the movement of the Spirit. Our movements, grounded in love, ought to overflow and spill out of containers, be messy, take up space and create it.

Where could this kind of courageous change take us as a church into a future of flourishing? I can see it now: millennia of people finding their way through uncertain present and future, showing up for each other, sustaining themselves in grief and love and song, getting lost along the way in the pull of empire, the pull of power that beckons with comfort and privilege and safety. And resisting this pull, coming back to a knowledge of belovedness, of fierce belonging created for self and others.

Pastor and theologian Steph Chandler Burns writes about how they learned about the nature of God from their grandmother, who actively worked to create welcome for LGBTQ2S+ people: "God is a grandmother," writes Chandler Burns. "She is fiercely loving of her grandchildren and stands up to anyone who would exclude them. More than anything, she wants her beloved grandchildren to thrive in a church that loves them as much as she does."[11]

Embracing fierce grandmother love, I hope that with my fellow sojourners in this church movement we can keep the boundaries looser, embrace the grey areas, live with the unresolved questions and ambiguities, always centering ourselves around an ethic of life and well-being for all. May we act, love, and live our way forward into a deep knowing of the divine in ourselves, in others, in the natural world, in all the places where God is at work healing, renewing, restoring.

This is the story of faith I want to live in, to originate from, to work toward. An evolving, embracing kind of faith that sees the value in each life, human, plant, or animal, in our interconnected world. A faith practiced together in communities large and small, moving beyond individuals to an interconnected ecosystem of mutually reinforcing groups and organizations saying and living out the belief that life is precious, is beloved of God, in all its manifestations.

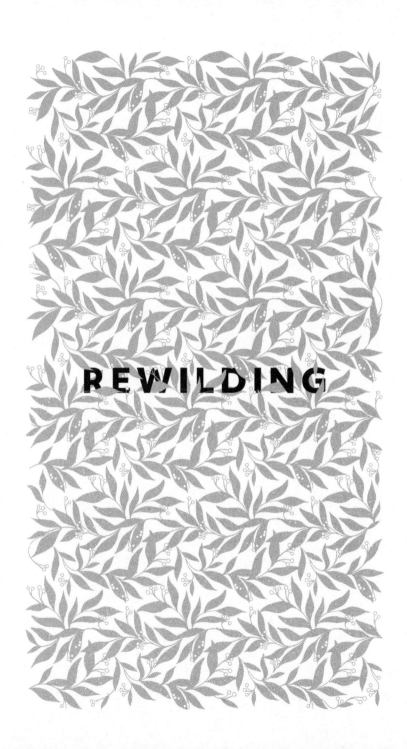

REWILDING

REWILDING AND PLANTING SEEDS FOR TOMORROW

Periwinkle, goutweed, and garlic mustard are the unholy trinity of my urban yard's flora. Each year, periwinkle's glossy green vines with purple flowers encroach on more and more of the space between the hedge (now trimmed to a bylaw-compliant height) hemming in our corner lot and the beginning of the grassy area. I pull out as many vines as I can reach, filling up paper bags of yard waste.

I've mostly given up on the goutweed. One year I tried covering it with garbage bags to smother it, but the patches were so resilient they pushed out the edges and grew up anyway, spreading to other areas. Once or twice a summer I rip out the creeping goutweed stems, pulling them away from the hostas and ferns so that these plants, which I actually want growing in my garden, can grow and thrive.

I've made the most progress with garlic mustard. When we moved into this house, a 1910 brick two-story house in urban Kitchener, Ontario, the garlic mustard had been left unchecked, growing as tall as my waist in the neglected strip between the wall of the house and the neighbor's driveway. European immigrants brought garlic mustard with them to be an early spring edible green, a critical source of vitamin C after a long winter. Here in the southern Ontario ecosystem, garlic mustard grows quickly, and few creatures eat it. Its pungent roots contaminate the soil and poison other plants around it. Where garlic mustard has escaped into forested areas, it pushes out the native spring ephemerals—the trilliums, bloodroot, and bluebells that offer early spring sustenance to pollinator species. The formerly untamed garlic mustard patch in my yard is now a patch of raspberries and strawberries, thriving in the warmth that the bricks soak up from the southern sun exposure at the side of the house. There are peonies and hydrangeas I transplanted from my aunt's garden for their lush blooms. A profusion of orange daylilies claims more space every year, despite my attempts to keep them contained to one area. A sage plant, leaves soft to the touch, draws bees of all shapes and sizes to the purple columns of blossom. I plant zinnias and marigolds in the garden box with the perennial herbs and let milkweed grow out front, hoping for monarch visitors. I plant packets of wildflower seeds and cuttings from friends and neighbors. On occasion, I splurge and buy a few annuals for extra zing and color.

Season by season, I'm tending and transforming this space. I have a vision for what I hope it will look like—more native species, a mix of blooms throughout the season, wild around the edges but also with tame space for grass and patio areas. Each year, though, it turns out a bit different. One year, bright yellow black-eyed Susans grew profusely. This year, in the same wildflower patch, phlox did well, with no black-eyed Susans in sight. Periwinkle still tries to push its way into every open space, but the wild strawberry ground cover I planted is thriving and pushing it back.

My garden is a holy place for me. Walking around barefoot in the grass, getting my hands into the dirt, tending the edges a handful of weeds at a time helps me feel connected to God, to the intricacies of creation, and to the spark of life that flows through it all. It's a tangible reminder that I am part of the miracle that life exists on this planet in the depths of the universe, where so far we know of no other life beyond what is here. Spending time in the garden also grounds me in my family's historical connection to land, and to the generations of ancestors who took part in these activities before me. My house and yard as a whole may not rise to the upkeep standards of my great-grandparents Orla and Catherine, but I like to think they would have loved the flowers. Especially the peonies.

Spending time outdoors tending to the land and its abundance also keeps me mindful of the original caretakers of this land, and my responsibilities to care for the land and creatures and live in respect and mutuality with all nations here. The ground I tend is part of the Haldimand Tract, land promised to the Six Nations of the Grand River. Land for which they have not been paid according to the treaty agreement, and land that generations of my ancestors as well as I have benefited from financially. The sacrament of tending my garden is also holy to me for this lived call for repentance, a physical experience that calls me into my responsibilities over and over to work with others to build shared power for change and repair of harm.

It feels like a tiny act of faith every time I plant a seed into this sacred ground and hope that it will grow, trusting in the nourishing darkness of the soil built up over millennia and which I, too, nourish with compost and mulch. I love that Jesus thought and spoke in gardening and farming metaphors too. There are so many parables about seeds and tending fruit. Jesus was carefully attuned to the rhythms and patterns of nature and the cycle of the seasons.

I'm not alone in seeking change through the small choices of gardening. When I walk around my neighborhood, I see gardens of pollinator-friendly poppies and coneflowers. Another house has replaced a front patch of grass with mosses and low-growing succulents. A southwest facing house uses the whole front yard for year-round vegetable production, with plastic tunnels for growing kale and chard through the winter. A project in my community brought Indigenous organizations together with residents to plant native species in a local park, part of a rewilding initiative to help local pollinator species and preserve biodiversity while also building relationships toward reconciliation.

Rewilding is a method from conservation biology that seeks to create conditions for ecosystems to maintain balance and thrive, increasing biodiversity and restoring damaged areas to their natural, uncultivated state. While there are some hopes at the outset for how a rewilded ecosystem might develop, variables like weather affect what thrives or doesn't. An ecosystem can be influenced, but not controlled. It's wild.

The ideas shared in this book suggest a path forward for creating the conditions for a future of flourishing, recognizing that we don't know what the outcomes of these faith, leadership, and culture shifts will be. There are many visions of flourishing, and the future we are working toward is not about promoting one vision but about creating space for many visions of flourishing to emerge from the diversity of human experience. Just as rewilding is a practice of resetting the balance of an ecosystem, this book aims for a reset of values, beliefs, and practices to move toward a healthier future in which more life can thrive. In thinking about what a healthier future looks like, each of us will inevitably come to a different answer, unique to our experiences, needs, and situations. There are many possible visions for futures of flourishing.

Courageous change depends on imagination. The future is always being dreamed into being. The question is, Whose dream for the future are you living in your daily life actions? Where does that dream come from? We can't change our lives, our communities, our world, and the patterns of relationships in it unless we first imagine new stories of what a good life could be and how we might find our way there together—and then listen to each other's imagined good futures. And then we can dream some more. This is the power of futurist fiction, dystopian fiction, sci-fi and fantasy stories; freed from the constrictions of the world as it is, we are invited into new stories that test out other ways of being, new patterns of relations. Whether in movies and TV, novels, or theater, stories offer a set of values and assumptions. Sometimes these reinforce the dominant narratives. Other times they tender a new story of how relations between people and our world could be.

Science fiction writer Octavia Butler was deeply skilled at this craft. In an essay called "A Few Rules for Predicting the Future," Butler recalls a conversation with a student who wanted to know the answer to all the suffering in the world, the troubles that Butler predicts in her near-future dystopian novels. There is no answer, she says, and then elaborates: "I mean there's no single answer that will solve all of our future problems. There's no magic bullet. Instead there are thousands of answers—at least. You can be one of them if you choose to be."[1]

Butler emphasizes that both she and her main characters place hope at the center, even and especially in challenging contexts when the future looks grim. "The very act of trying to look ahead to discern possibilities and offer warnings is in itself an act of hope."[2]

This rewilding of vision, of imagination, is an act of hope. It is a journey of action, of moving forward with others in the struggle to imagine different, better futures. Whether we gain or lose ground in the struggles, the courageous community we build together along the way is stronger for it. It is tending a better tomorrow simply in the act of coming together to create change in the ways we can.

This spring, I watched the black-and-white flashes of two chickadees flit in and out of the wooden birdhouse in the Japanese lilac tree in our yard, the early leaf buds signaling the start of a new season of nest building.

Now what do we need, the chickadees trilled. *Now what? Now how do we make this our home? Can this be our home? What do we need to make this our home?*

How do we make this world our home, in the mess of it all? What twigs, old strings, and dried grasses will we turn into something beautiful and hospitable in the unknowable future?

While the smoke swirls from the wildfires that now seem to be a fixture of summer weather in Canada, I'm tending my strawberry patch. My spouse Luke is taking Ava on evening bike rides to get her off training wheels so all four of us can travel more by bicycle. We decided to plant a tulip tree, a fast-growing, tall species native to our Carolinian forest landscape, in our yard to increase the neighborhood tree canopy coverage and to help pollinators. I've been teaching Isaac the names of flowers and herbs, and by now he's often better than me at identifying birds in our yard. We're piecing together a nest of small, beautiful things to keep us living in hope, pushing past the apathy and despair to work at the kind of courageous change we need for a livable future.

Octavia Butler's words echo in my head: "Our tomorrow is the child of our today. Through thought and deed, we exert a great deal of influence over this child, even though we can't control it absolutely. Best to think about it, though. Best to try to shape it into something good. Best to do that for any child."[3]

We tend to these small changes in our yards and community garden plots and apartment balconies—metaphorical and physical—not because they solve the great problems we face, but because in tending the small changes, we strengthen ourselves, building up muscles of joy and resistance to imagine that a different world is possible. Twig by twig, we keep building and rebuilding, making this changing world our home.

EPILOGUE

Dear Ava

Dear Ava Hope,

At your baby dedication we read "Hope Is the Thing with Feathers," the old words from Emily Dickinson come to life in you. The meaning of your name, Ava, is linked to the Latin word for bird, *avis*. I pray that you hold on to your songs, your love of color and brightness, your fierce determination. Use them to keep the thing with feathers singing inside you even as the storms rage on. You will need courage and perseverance on your life journey, and there will be times the despair overwhelms you. I know you will also find and create beauty, joy, and connection no matter the twists and turns in your road ahead.

What a time to be born, at a juncture when we know without doubt the absolute power of humans to impact the earth. Yet we are humbled again and again by creatures as minute as the virus invaders replicating in our cells. We are humbled to be alive in this briefest of moments in the cosmic history of the universe, of our galaxy spun into being, of our sun forming and this celestial orb we call home melded and molded out of stardust from the origins of time and space. A blink of Creator's eye holds our species' entire history of love and grief, stories and song, loss and discovery, pain and hope.

What a time to be born, carrying in your body the lingering memory of ocean tides and primordial ancestors while contemplating what our present human existence is doing to sea creatures, coral reefs, and the coasts out of which our ocean-dwelling forebears emerged on the journey to the peoplehood of our species.

In the dinosaur book I read your older brother daily for a year, there is a photograph of a feathered tail preserved in amber. The texture of the feathers' branches encased in translucent gold looks like the soft tail feather of a sparrow that you picked up from the grass under the willow tree. The world of the sparrow's ancestor lingers in hints, reminding us that we are here now but may not always be. Scientists name this period in which we live the Anthropocene, the period in which human activity has started to change the earth's climate and ecosystems. Which humans? Which activities? Whose lives, bodies, land bear the scars, and who owns the spoils? The questions echo across the generations.

When I was pregnant with you, I had a moment of deep recognition that I was carrying you and the eggs in your fetal ovaries that may someday become my grandchildren, knowing that part of who I am and now who you are was once part of the eggs in my mother's body carried in my maternal grandmother's body. From my grandmother to your potential children, we are connected together, shaped and changed by the environment around us from generation to generation. What my grandma Doris ate, the stresses she experienced, the environment around her—all of this is now part of who you and I are today, embedded in our bodies. Who you are, who you are becoming, is connected even further to the past with hidden and visible ties, the line of ancestors behind us and their influence on who we are stretching back to the original moment of cosmic creation, in the star matter that formed the elements in our human bodies. The industrial cleaning product fumes from the office in the basement of the supportive housing building where I worked during the fall of 2018 while pregnant with you in Kitchener, Ontario, and the peaches from Huffman's Fruit Farm in Salem, Ohio, that Grandma Doris ate in the summer of 1954, and the carbon expelled in a supernova star explosion thirteen or fourteen billion years ago: all are part of who you are and what you carry forward in your life on this planet.

I hope that you can remember you are so small, so infinitesimally tiny in the great big universe, and that you are so, so deeply beloved and known by your Creator, down to the atoms and their orbiting electrons and quarks that make up the foundational pieces of who you are; that you know in your being you belong here in the community of the cosmos in this time and place. You need to know this—that your belovedness now in the Anthropocene and the belovedness of a sparrow-tailed dinosaur from the Mesozoic Era are never in question, that your Creator made you and pronounced you good.

Remember the belovedness of your kindergarten classmates and the rainbow of colors, cultures, and languages that you formed onstage together singing a Raffi song at your school concert. Remember the belovedness of our unhoused neighbors living in the tent clusters that are now hallmarks of our city. Remember the belovedness of all genders, including yours, as you grow into who you are meant to be and to love who you love. Remember the belovedness of monarch butterflies, and eastern tiger salamanders, Acadian flycatchers, and pale-bellied frost lichen, and each member of the community of creation that makes up our shared world. Embed this knowing of belovedness in your DNA, make it part of you, so that it can fuel you through the grief, loss, and pain of what it means to be human, and especially what it means to be human in this time of unprecedented loss of natural and cultural heritage. I hope you know, too, that grief is the other side of belovedness. You have to feel love to feel grief, to mourn the loss of something or someone precious to you, precious to God.

What will your future look like? What kind of world are you inheriting? What will your place be in it? The world is better already because you are present in it, bringing your laughter and spark and joy, and your intense drive to make your ideas reality. Much of what we know or thought we knew is crumbling like an old clay pot in our hands. All our futures are uncertain in the face of climate chaos and rising global tides of political and economic volatility. But life has always been uncertain. That is part of the package of embodied human existence, and it's easier for some than others, though no one escapes without suffering.

What I thought I knew about the nature of trees and of fungi was turned on its head when I learned that webs of fungi—mycorrhizal networks—connect the roots of trees to each other, allowing them to share information, water, and nutrients through the whole system so that the whole forest can thrive together. The mushrooms that pop up out of nowhere are the fruit of a long-established underground system of interconnections. My hope, in the face of the uncertainty ahead, is for you to build a wide network of relationships around you, for your own support and for the support of others. That you will rise up into view when needed, propelled by a vast web of invisible connections that support the flourishing of the whole. Give time to these relationships, to tending a community of belovedness, so that you know you are not alone even when you feel it most. Like the fairy ring mushrooms that appear on the forest floor out of the underground organism when the time is right, I hope you stand up and speak up, rising to the occasion along with others and supported from below as you blossom.

Our ancestors, in Canada and the United States, came to this continent from Europe fueled by stories of repression and persecution, powered by a desire to practice a simple faith and live the kind of rural, peaceful life they valued. They loved the land, knew in their bones that farming is holy work. What is also true is they were invited to the United States and later to Upper Canada because the British Empire saw them as ideal actors for settler colonialism, willing to cut down forests for farm fields without asking hard questions about who the land belonged to before they arrived. They were the Germanic Christian "quiet in the land" who would do the heavy lifting to build roads and settlements and meetinghouses and produce food to further the colonial project that built the country we live in today, in which Indigenous Peoples are still pushed to the margins of land and society. This is our history, too, part of the legacy that has shaped you and me and brought us here to this time and place. We have to hold it all together, the good and the bad mixed up as they always are in the messy reality of being human. We have to find the courage to step into responsibility and into new growth, the possibility of learning and change.

Somewhere in our family and faith history are also the seeds of peace and justice. Seeds of seeking to show love to enemies, and of believing that Jesus' call to peace was meant to be taken literally. That is also part of what we have inherited. An essay in the Reesor family genealogy book traces our physical and spiritual ancestors back to 1400s Switzerland. Our ancestors were part of the Waldensian Christian movement that valued simple living, the direct reading of Scripture, and the priesthood of all believers. Just imagine, these seeds that shape how we live our lives in the world today were planted more than five hundred years ago, longer ago even than that.

I am trying my best to keep planting and tending these seeds within you, within our family and our community. I want to add to them seeds of kinship with creation, seeds of transparency and repentance, seeds of resistance and action for transforming injustice that harms the belovedness of people and creation.

The thing about seeds is you just don't know how they're going to grow. Or even if they are going to grow at all. It takes care and tending and faith in the unseen magic of germination that happens in the dark. Some seeds, like birch tree seeds, need to experience a season of cold in order to sprout. Others can lay dormant for years until the right conditions unleash their potential. And some seeds seem to grow without ceasing, coming up in compost piles and sidewalk cracks, their enthusiasm to burst into the world unquenchable.

As you grow up, you and your brother and your kindergarten classmates and your global generation of children born into this world in crisis, I hope the seeds of well-being, the seeds of liberation, of shalom for people and all creation, can take root in your good soil. And I hope you find the courage and hope to plant seeds of your own. I know you can tend these seeds into something beautiful: something needed, something wild and flourishing to shape beautiful tomorrows.

ACKNOWLEDGMENTS

Books are best written in community, and I'm grateful for the many people who have supported and encouraged me along the way.

The Kindred Credit Union Centre for Peace Advancement welcomed me as Writer-in-Residence during the drafting of this manuscript. Thank you to staff and affiliates, especially Paul Heidebrecht, Teresa Edge, Joey Ou, Fatoumatta Camara, Sophia Petitt, Majid Mizra, and everyone who took part in coffee break discussions.

Thank you to Laureen Harder-Gissing and the staff at Milton Good Library/Mennonite Archives of Ontario at Conrad Grebel University College for helping me access research and archival materials, even when I said vague things like "I'm looking for a large brown book with Reesor in the title."

Thank you to Khaadeeja Motiwala and Omar El-Gamal for sharing their astrophysics expertise.

Kathryn Lymburner has been more of an "alpha to omega" reader than a beta reader, though she is that too. I'm grateful for her early editing work on my proposal as well as writing pep talks all along the way.

I'm grateful to Rebecca Janzen for early chapter comments, writing accountability and moral support, and for sharing your contagious love of history and archival research with me.

Thank you to Kimberley Penner, for the book writing meetups that turned into generative conversations instead, and for responding to my theology emergencies.

Steph Chandler Burns gave me my first queer theology reading list over coffee. Michiko Bown-Kai introduced me to theologian Austen Hartke's writing in their 2023 Beyond Binaries conference keynote address.

I'm indebted to those who reviewed and gave me feedback on chapter drafts: Nathan Funk, Jamie Pitts, Samuel Steiner, Christen Kong, and Hyung Jin Kim Sun.

A number of groups and churches heard early versions of chapters in sermons and presentations: Thank you to Silver Lake Mennonite Camp's Women's Retreat participants, Rockway Mennonite Collegiate chapel participants, Erb Street Mennonite Church, Stirling Avenue Mennonite Church, and Markham Chinese Mennonite Church for your warm reception and feedback.

Thank you to the Junia Centre co-dreamers for helping me imagine what change could look like. Junia Centre's story is still being written, and I'm glad to be writing it together with you.

I'm grateful to the whole Herald Press team, especially acquisitions editor Laura Leonard and editor Sara Versluis who caught the vision for this book from the beginning and helped it become the best version of itself. Thank you!

Finally, I could not have done this without the unwavering support of my family. I'm grateful to my parents Miriam and Jay Reesor for doing lots of babysitting and bringing meals so that I could keep on writing to meet deadlines. I'm also grateful for their enthusiastic responses to being some of the first readers of the whole book. My children Isaac and Ava for maybe not understanding, but accepting, when I spent weekend and vacation time writing. To my spouse Luke—you're the throughline in this book, and in my life.

QUESTIONS FOR DISCUSSION

CHAPTER 1: REDREAMING AT THE ROOTS

1. When you think about the year 2100, what do you imagine the world will be like?
2. Many books talk about what we should do to combat climate change. This book looks at who we are and how we want to be in relation to a world in flux. In your life and in your faith community or organizations, do you think more about what you should do or about how you want to be?

CHAPTER 2: RETELLING FAMILY AND SPIRITUAL ANCESTRY STORIES

1. When you think about your family history or your faith history, what do you want to take with you? What do you want to leave behind?
2. What do you want to learn more about your family history or faith history?
3. What is the history of the land you are on? From past to present, who else has called this land home?

CHAPTER 3: RETELLING CREATION STORIES

1. The author describes how learning about Indigenous and queer theology changed her views on the role of people in creation from hierarchical to interconnected and interdependent. What has influenced your views on the role of people in relation to creation?

2. Does understanding how rare and precious life is in the vast, unknowable universe make you feel more or less sacred?

3. How might people think or act differently if we understand ourselves to have a duty to live in harmony with the natural world instead of understanding ourselves to have a responsibility to be good stewards of the earth and its resources? What is different about these two perspectives? Which one are you most drawn to?

CHAPTER 4: RENEWING OUR HOPE AND TRANSFORMING DESPAIR

1. How do you define hope?

2. In your own life, how do you keep the dangers of despair, apathy, and cynicism at bay?

3. Have you ever seen overoptimism lead to apathy? What did this look like? Why do you think this happened?

4. Think about the people, things, and experiences that you feel grief for. What does your grief tell you about your values and hopes?

CHAPTER 5: REIMAGINING LEADERSHIP

1. In your place of work, worship, or elsewhere in your community, how do you see leadership modeled?

2. Are you already being intentional, or could you be, about experiencing leadership in different forms, and

from people whom you're not used to experiencing leadership from?

3. The author argues that the climate crisis can be understood as a leadership crisis. Do you agree or disagree with this assertion? Why so?

CHAPTER 6: REIMAGINING COMMUNITY

1. Look up a power mapping exercise, assessing sources of power in your own community groups. The Power Flower Exercise from the We Rise Toolkit, available online, is one example.

2. What values, beliefs, and practices undergird the culture of your congregation, workplace, or family? Are these similar to or different from what you see expressed in your broader cultural context?

CHAPTER 7: REIMAGINING ACCOUNTABILITY AND REPAIRING HARM

1. How does perfectionism show up in your life? How does it show up in your community?

2. Think about a time you received hard feedback well. What made you feel safe enough to receive the feedback without getting defensive?

CHAPTER 8: REIMAGINING CHURCH AS MOVEMENT

1. If you consider yourself to be part of a church or other faith community, what images or metaphors do you find helpful to describe it?

2. Movements are made up of a variety of components that can be formal and informal, like organizations, institutions, neighborhood groups, artists, media, and

writers. What movements do you consider yourself to be part of, if any?

3. How are the faith communities and organizations or other groups that you are part of connected to bigger visions, coalitions, or movements?

4. Are you part of any groups or faith communities that are taking action related to climate change? What is your unique contribution to this global challenge?

CHAPTER 9: REWILDING AND PLANTING SEEDS FOR TOMORROW

1. This book explores many seeds of beliefs, values, and practices that can have intended and unintended effects on the present and the future. What seeds are you trying to plant in your life, in your community, and in the world right now?

2. When you think of what a good, flourishing future of well-being for people and the planet looks like, what do you imagine? What do others imagine?

3. Where can you learn about and support other people's ideas of the "good life"?

EPILOGUE: DEAR AVA

1. This essay in the form of a personal letter to the author's child contains her family and origin story and the values that the author hopes to pass down to her children and other descendants. What might you write to a younger person?

2. What wisdom do you hope to pass on to help guide future generations? Who has passed wisdom and family stories on to you? How have they done so?

NOTES

PREFACE

1. Timothy K. Beal, *When Time Is Short: Finding Our Way in the Anthropocene* (Boston: Beacon Press, 2022), 5–6.

2. The Anabaptist movement began in the 1500s, part of the Radical Reformation in Europe. Today, Anabaptist groups include Mennonites, Amish, Hutterites, Church of the Brethren, Brethren in Christ, Mennonite Brethren, and more. When referencing the larger movement, I follow the lead of Mennonite World Conference, a global communing body of Christian churches rooted in the Anabaptist movement, which uses the term Anabaptist-Mennonite. When referring to a particular strand of Anabaptism or to a church denomination, I use the relevant term, such as Mennonite Church Canada or Brethren in Christ. When referring to an ethnocultural group that has links to Anabaptism, I use terms such as Swiss Mennonite.

3. Hyung Jin Kim Sun, "Intercultural Global Theology," *Vision: A Journal for Church and Theology* 19, no. 2 (Fall 2018): 83.

4. Kim Sun, 84.

CHAPTER 1

1. Intergovernmental Panel on Climate Change, *Global Warming of 1.5°C: IPCC Special Report on Impacts of Global Warming of 1.5°C above Pre-Industrial Levels in Context of Strengthening Response to Climate Change, Sustainable Development, and Efforts to Eradicate Poverty*, 1st ed. (Cambridge University Press, 2022), https://doi.org/10.1017/9781009157940.

2. UNICEF, *The Climate Crisis Is a Child Rights Crisis: Introducing the Children's Climate Risk Index* (New York: UNICEF, 2021), 6, 15.

3. adrienne maree brown, *Emergent Strategy: Shaping Change, Changing Worlds* (Chico, CA: AK Press, 2017), 53.

CHAPTER 2

1. Meera Subramanian, "Humans versus Earth: The Quest to Define the Anthropocene," *Nature* 572, no. 7768 (August 2019): 168–70, https://doi.org/10.1038/d41586-019-02381-2.

2. "Crawford Lake Studies," *Conservation Halton* (blog), last modified December 28, 2023, https://www.conservationhalton.ca/crawford-lake-studies/.

3. Subramanian, "Humans versus Earth."

4. Françoise Vergès, "Racial Capitalocene: Is the Anthropocene Racial?," *Verso* (blog), August 30, 2017, https://www.versobooks.com/en-ca/blogs/news/3376-racial-capitalocene.

5. "The Geology of Southern Ontario," ArcGIS StoryMaps, June 2, 2023, https://storymaps.arcgis.com/collections/80c3ac91abc5451ca23cd16c85f0dfe4.

6. Kelly E. Hayes and Mariame Kaba, *Let This Radicalize You: Organizing and the Revolution of Reciprocal Care*, Abolitionist Papers (Chicago: Haymarket, 2023), 3.

7. The Reesor Family in Canada website (ReesorFamily.on.ca) gives the date as 1796. No exact date is known, and Samuel J. Steiner suggests this did not happen at all. Steiner, *In Search of Promised Lands: A Religious History of Mennonites in Ontario*, Studies of Anabaptist and Mennonite History 48 (Harrisonburg, VA: Herald Press, 2015), 613n54.

8. Six Nations Lands and Resources Department, "Land Rights: A Global Solution for the Six Nations of the Grand River," Impact Assessment Agency of Canada, last modified July 12, 2019, https://iaac-aeic.gc.ca/050/documents/p80100/130877E.pdf.

9. Six Nations Lands and Resources Department, "Land Rights."

10. Steiner, *In Search of Promised Lands*, 613n54.

11. Six Nations Lands and Resources Department, "Land Rights."

12. Steiner, *In Search of Promised Lands*, 72–74.

13. "The Rouge Tract Claim Submitted in 2015," Mississaugas of the Credit First Nation, November 5, 2020, https://mncfn.ca/the-rouge-tract-claim-submitted-in-2015/.

14. There are many perspectives on the history and significance of the Dish with One Spoon. My learning has been shaped by Leanne Simpson, "Looking after Gdoo-Naaganinaa: Precolonial Nishnaabeg Diplomatic and Treaty Relationships," *Wicazo Sa Review* 23, no. 2 (2008): 29–42, https://doi.org/10.1353/wic.0.0001; and Dean M. Jacobs and Victor P. Lytwyn, "Naagan Ge Bezhig Emkwaan: A Dish with One Spoon Reconsidered," *Ontario History* 112, no. 2 (October 14, 2020): 191–210, https://doi.org/10.7202/1072237ar.

15. Simpson, "Looking after Gdoo-Naaganinaa," 37.

16. Simpson, 36.

17. "The Geology of Southern Ontario," ArcGIS StoryMaps.

18. "About MWC," Mennonite World Conference, last modified July 25, 2023, https://mwc-cmm.org/en/about-mwc.

19. Robyn Maynard and Leanne Betasamosake Simpson, *Rehearsals for Living*, Abolitionist Papers (Chicago: Haymarket, 2022).

20. Dionne Brand, *Bread Out of Stone: Recollections on Sex, Recognitions, Race, Dreaming and Politics*, rev. ed. (Toronto: Vintage Canada, 1998), 136.

21. Robin Wall Kimmerer, *Braiding Sweetgrass: Indigenous Wisdom, Scientific Knowledge, and the Teachings of Plants* (Minneapolis: Milkweed Editions, 2013).

CHAPTER 3

1. Office of Science, "DOE Explains . . . Supernovae," US Department of Energy, accessed August 3, 2023, https://www.energy.gov/science/doe-explainssupernovae.

2. "Dark Energy, Dark Matter," NASA, June 10, 2007, https://science.nasa.gov/astrophysics/focus-areas/what-is-dark-energy.

3. William Brighty Rands, "Great, Wide, Beautiful, Wonderful World," originally published in W. B. Rand, *Lilliput Lyrics*, ed. R. Brimley Johnson (London: John Lane, the Bodley Head, 1899): 101–2. Available at https://rpo.library.utoronto.ca/content/great-wide-beautiful-wonderful-world.

4. Jason Arunn Murugesu, "We Now Know How Many Cells There Are in the Human Body," *New Scientist*, September 18, 2023, https://www.newscientist.com/article/2392685-we-now-know-how-many-cells-there-are-in-the-human-body/.

5. Lynn White, "The Historical Roots of Our Ecologic Crisis," *Science* 155, no. 3767 (March 10, 1967): 1203–7, https://doi.org/10.1126/science.155.3767.1203.

6. Rosemary Radford Ruether, *Gaia and God: An Ecofeminist Theology of Earth Healing*, 1st ed. (San Francisco: HarperSanFrancisco, 1992), 15.

7. Wayne Grudem, *Systematic Theology* (Grand Rapids: Zondervan, 1994), 266, 273.

8. "How Many Earths? How Many Countries?," Overshoot, last modified August 3, 2023, https://overshoot.footprintnetwork.org/how-many-earths-or-countries-do-we-need/.

9. Sierra Ross Richer, "Climate Pollinator Story 46: It Starts with Language," Anabaptist Climate Collective, last modified June 21, 2023, https://www.anabaptistclimate.org/climate-pollinator-series/nx954pnrtscsct5-a58gm-hgjr8-w57jr-m2rwl-lk666-nweyp-bg3j9-5efmn-2a3nd-x83m9-s3w97-xweyp-6wc46-f4zj4-yb2eb-a5ljm-mnt6s.

10. Robin Wall Kimmerer, *Braiding Sweetgrass: Indigenous Wisdom, Scientific Knowledge and the Teachings of Plants* (Minneapolis: Milkweed Editions, 2013), 55.

11. Robin Wall Kimmerer, "Speaking of Nature," *Orion*, June 12, 2017, https://orionmagazine.org/article/speaking-of-nature/.

12. Sierra Ross Richer, "Climate Pollinator Story 48: *Ayni*: An Invitation and a Vision," Anabaptist Climate Collective, last modified June 21, 2023, https://www.anabaptistclimate.org/climate-pollinator-series/nx954pnrtscsct5-a58gm-hgjr8-w57jr-m2rwl-lk666-nweyp-bg3j9-5efmn-2a3nd-x83m9-s3w97-xweyp-6wc46-f4zj4-yb2eb-a5ljm-mnt6s-l4zzw-kfpkn.

13. Randy Woodley, *Shalom and the Community of Creation: An Indigenous Vision*, Prophetic Christianity (Grand Rapids: Eerdmans, 2012).

14. Austen Hartke, *Transforming: The Bible and the Lives of Transgender Christians* (Louisville: Westminster John Knox, 2018), 48, 53.

15. Alie Ward, "Astrobiology (ALIENS) with Dr. Kevin Peter Hand," *Ologies Podcast*, March 18, 2019, https://www.alieward.com/ologies/astrobiology?rq=astrobiology.

16. Stephanie Pappas, "Why Has a Group of Orcas Suddenly Started Attacking Boats?," *Scientific American*, May 24, 2023, https://www.scientificamerican.com/article/why-has-a-group-of-orcas-suddenly-started-attacking-boats/.

17. Andrew Adamatzky, "Language of Fungi Derived from Their Electrical Spiking Activity," *Royal Society Open Science* 9, no. 4 (April 2022): 211926, https://doi.org/10.1098/rsos.211926.

CHAPTER 4

1. International Centre for Integrated Mountain Development et al., *Glacial Lakes and Glacial Lake Outburst Floods in Nepal* (Kathmandu: International Centre for Integrated Mountain Development, 2011), 7.

2. Philippus Wester, Sunita Chaudhary, Nakul Chettri, Miriam Jackson, Amina Maharjan, Santosh Nepal, and Jakob F. Steiner, eds., *Water, Ice, Society, and Ecosystems in the Hindu Kush Himalaya: An Outlook* (International Centre for Integrated Mountain Development, 2023), vi, https://doi.org/10.53055/ICIMOD.1028.

3. Caroline Hickman et al., "Climate Anxiety in Children and Young People and Their Beliefs about Government Responses to Climate Change: A Global Survey," *Lancet Planetary Health* 5, no. 12 (December 2021): e863–73, https://doi.org/10.1016/S2542-5196(21)00278-3.

4. Nancy Elizabeth Bedford, *Who Was Jesus and What Does It Mean to Follow Him?*, The Jesus Way: Small Books of Radical Faith (Harrisonburg, VA: Herald Press, 2021).

5. Galen Peters and Robert A. Riall, eds., *The Earliest Hymns of the Ausbund: Some Beautiful Christian Songs Composed and Sung in the Prison at Passau, Published in 1564*, Anabaptist Texts in Translation 3 (Kitchener, ON: Pandora Press; Scottdale, PA: Herald Press, 2003), 21.

6. Peters and Riall, 83.

7. Robert Friedman, "Ausbund," *Global Anabaptist Mennonite Encyclopedia Online*, January 15, 2017, https://gameo.org/index.php?title=Ausbund&oldid=144754.

8. C. Arnold Snyder, *Anabaptist History and Theology: Revised Student Edition* (Kitchener: Pandora Press, 1997), 79–183.

9. Joanna Macy and Chris Johnstone, *Active Hope: How to Face the Mess We're In with Unexpected Resilience and Creative Power*, rev. ed. (Novato, CA: New World Library, 2022), 63.

10. Bedford, *Who Was Jesus*, 71.

11. Kelly E. Hayes and Mariame Kaba, *Let This Radicalize You: Organizing and the Revolution of Reciprocal Care*, Abolitionist Papers (Chicago: Haymarket, 2023), 176–77.

CHAPTER 5

1. Suzanne Simard, *Finding the Mother Tree: Discovering the Wisdom of the Forest* (Toronto: Allen Lane, 2021).

2. Moisés Naím, *The Revenge of Power: How Autocrats Are Reinventing Politics for the 21st Century*, 1st ed. (New York: St. Martin's Press, 2022), 44.

3. Rachel Thomas et al., "Women in the Workplace Report" (New York: McKinsey; Palo Alto: LeanIn.org, 2022), 8, 13, 17, https://womenintheworkplace.com/Women_in_the_Workplace_2022.pdf.

4. Amy Diehl, Leanne M. Dzubinski, and Amber L. Stephenson, "Women in Leadership Face Ageism at Every Age," *Harvard Business Review*, June 16, 2023, https://hbr.org/2023/06/women-in-leadership-face-ageism-at-every-age.

5. Heather Russek, Jessica Thornton, and Camara Chambers, *Embracing Our Future: Social Purpose Leadership in 2030* (Toronto: Creative Futures and Leadership Lab, 2022), 2, 6, https://dais.ca/reports/embracing-our-future-social-purpose-leadership-in-2030/.

6. Kate Graham, *No Second Chances: Women and Political Power in Canada* (Toronto: Second Story Press, 2022), 5.

7. Ayana Elizabeth Johnson and Katharine K. Wilkinson, eds., *All We Can Save: Truth, Courage, and Solutions for the Climate Crisis* (New York: One World, 2020).

8. John Paul Lederach, "On Mass and Movement: The Theory of the Critical Yeast," *The Moral Imagination: The Art and Soul of Building Peace* (New York: Oxford University Press, 2005), 89, https://doi.org/10.1093/0195174542.003.0009.

9. Alÿcia Bacon, "The Path of the Warrior: Elizabeth Yeampierre—On Organizing and the Future of the Diaspora," *Transition* 133 (2022): 33–53, muse.jhu.edu/article/876692.

10. "Welcome to UPROSE!," UPROSE, accessed February 17, 2024, from https://www.uprose.org.

11. Emily Cassidy, "How Nepal Regenerated Its Forests," NASA Earth Observatory, last modified April 25, 2023, https://earthobservatory.nasa.gov/images/150937/how-nepal-regenerated-its-forests.

CHAPTER 6

1. World Health Organization and WHO Patient Safety, eds., *WHO Guidelines on Hand Hygiene in Health Care: First Global Patient Safety Challenge Clean Care Is Safer Care* (Geneva: World Health Organization, 2009), 5, https://www.ncbi.nlm.nih.gov/books/NBK144001/.

2. Ed Yong, *I Contain Multitudes: The Microbes within Us and a Grander View of Life* (New York: Ecco, 2016), 23, 24, 84.

3. Quoted in Yong, 25.

4. Tobin Miller Shearer, *Daily Demonstrators: The Civil Rights Movement in Mennonite Homes and Sanctuaries* (Baltimore: Johns Hopkins University Press, 2010), https://doi.org/10.1353/book.482.

5. Papers from a groundbreaking summit on this topic are compiled in Elizabeth Yoder, ed., *Peace Theology and Violence against Women* (Elkhart, IN: Institute of Mennonite Studies, 1992).

6. Paulo Freire, *Pedagogy of the Oppressed*, 30th anniversary ed. (New York: Continuum, 2000), 79.

7. Freire, 60–61.

CHAPTER 7

1. "Geoengineering," Harvard's Solar Engineering Research Program, accessed December 3, 2023, https://geoengineering.environment.harvard.edu/geoengineering.

2. Britta Clark, "How to Argue about Solar Geoengineering," *Journal of Applied Philosophy* 40, no. 3 (July 2023): 505–20, https://doi.org/10.1111/japp.12643.

3. "COP27 Reaches Breakthrough Agreement on New 'Loss and Damage' Fund for Vulnerable Countries," United Nations Climate Change, November 20, 2022, https://unfccc.int/news/cop27-reaches-breakthrough-agreement-on-new-loss-and-damage-fund-for-vulnerable-countries.

4. See adrienne maree brown, *Emergent Strategy: Shaping Change, Changing Worlds* (Chico, CA: AK Press, 2017).

5. Thomas Curran and Andrew P. Hill, "Perfectionism Is Increasing over Time: A Meta-Analysis of Birth Cohort Differences from 1989 to 2016," *Psychological Bulletin* 145, no. 4 (April 2019): 410, https://doi.org/10.1037/bul0000138.

6. Desmond Tutu, *No Future without Forgiveness* (New York: Doubleday, 2000), 274.

7. Truth and Reconciliation Commission of Canada, *Honouring the Truth, Reconciling for the Future: Summary of the Final Report of the Truth and Reconciliation Commission of Canada* (Winnipeg: Truth and Reconciliation Commission of Canada, 2015).

8. For a discussion of Mennonite involvement in residential schools and day schools in Canada, see Melanie Kampen, "The Mennonite Peacemaker Myth: Reconciliation without Truth-Telling?," *Conrad Grebel Review* 37, no. 1 (2019): 42.

9. Clarence Cachagee and Seth Ratzlaff, *North Wind Man* (St. Catharines, ON: Gelassenheit Publications, 2023), xviii.

CHAPTER 8

1. Leah Reesor-Keller, "Installation Sermon" (MCEC Fall Gathering, Kitchener, Ontario, November 14, 2020); quoted in Kara Carter, "God's Story, Our Story: Telling, Re-telling, Re-storying" (PhD diss., Martin Luther College, 2022), 78, https://scholars.wlu.ca/etd/2480/.

2. Emily Charron, "Systems Mapping Reveals Interconnected Webs in the Church," *Grebel Now*, Spring 2022, https://uwaterloo.ca/grebel-now/grebel-now-spring-2022/feature/systems-mapping-reveals-interconnected-webs-church.

3. For a deep dive into the experience of MCEC congregations and leaders adapting to the post-Christendom context and seeking new paradigms, see Carter, "God's Story, Our Story."

4. Kelly E. Hayes and Mariame Kaba, *Let This Radicalize You: Organizing and the Revolution of Reciprocal Care*, Abolitionist Papers (Chicago: Haymarket, 2023), 12.

5. Andrew Faiz, "Why Over a Third of Canadians Now Claim to Have No Religion," *Broadview*, May 2, 2023, https://broadview.org/secularism-canada/.

6. Yonat Shimron, "Poll: Religious Attendance Is Shrinking but Those Who Remain Are Happy," Religion News Service, May 16, 2023, https://religionnews.com/2023/05/16/poll-religious-attendance-is-shrinking-but-those-who-remain-are-happy/.

7. Canadian Youth Summit Delegates, *Global Youth Summit National Project: 2022 Report* ([n.p.]: Mennonite Church Canada, 2022).

8. Quoted in Adelle M. Banks, "Documentary on Black Millennials Depicts Wide Range of Religion," Religion News Service, October 30, 2023, https://religionnews.com/2023/10/24/documentary-on-black-millennials-depicts-wide-range-of-religion-rebellion/.

9. Sharon Stein et al., "Gesturing Towards Decolonial Futures: Reflections on Our Learnings Thus Far," *Nordic Journal of Comparative and International Education (NJCIE)* 4, no. 1 (June 1, 2020): 51, https://doi.org/10.7577/njcie.3518.

10. Kylie Cheung, "Ruth Wilson Gilmore Says Freedom Is a Physical Place—But Can We Find It?," *Jezebel*, June 21, 2022, https://jezebel.com/ruth-wilson-gilmore-says-freedom-is-a-physical-place-bu-1849079415. Ruth Wilson Gilmore's simplified definition draws on her body of work over three decades, collected in *Abolition Geographies* (New York: Verso, 2022).

11. Steph Chandler Burns, "Grandmother God," *Vision: A Journal for Church and Theology* 24, no. 2 (Fall 2023): 93.

CHAPTER 9

1. Octavia Butler, "A Few Rules for Predicting the Future," *Essence*, June 2000, https://commongood.cc/reader/a-few-rules-for-predicting-the-future-by-octavia-e-butler/.

2. Butler.

3. Butler.

THE AUTHOR

Leah Reesor-Keller is a speaker, writer, and leadership consultant who helps churches and non-profits set vision and strategy for transformational change. During her tenure as executive minister of Mennonite Church Eastern Canada, she led a historic revisioning process for the largest conference in the Mennonite Church Canada denomination. She has nearly twenty years' experience working with faith-based and social justice organizations in Canada, Haiti, Jamaica, and Nepal. Leah holds an MA in development studies and a BA in political science and peace and conflict studies. She lives with her spouse and children in Kitchener, Ontario, where she is rewilding her urban yard one dandelion at a time. Learn more about Leah at www.leahreesorkeller.com.